Why Isn't God Nice?

CW00734803

Kurt Bruner is a graduate o
more than twenty books in
in the Lord of the Rings. A sp
with Open Doors Internati
worldwide. His free podcast t
www.kurtbruner.com.

"Kurt Bruner tackles the uncomfortable question every local pastor faces time and time again about why a loving God allows pain and suffering. This compelling book gives helpful perspectives and useful language for those often-repeated conversations."

– Steve Stroope, Senior Pastor, Lake Pointe Church, author,
Tribal Church

"Kurt Bruner says things that aren't polite to utter in church. As one who observes first-hand the persecution of Christians around the world, I welcome the chance to openly wrestle with God's hard words and actions."

– Al Janssen, co-author, *Secret Believers: What Happens When Muslims Believe in Christ*

"The toughest questions, rooted in unflinching reality, are met with pastoral grace, scriptural expertise and – into the bargain – literary erudition. Life's biggest quests require all the big names, and so Kurt herds Moses, David, Jesus and Paul in with Marlowe, Dante, Twain, Wilde and Lewis to give us the stepping stones over which to pass through the torrents of suffering. It's about time we had a book that refuses to paddle in the shallows with life's hardest issues, and invites us into the deeper currents of truth... and Love! Be warned – you will drown, unless God holds out a hand!"

– Dr Ronald Boyd-MacMillan, author of *Faith that Endures: the Essential Guide to the Persecuted Church*, and Director of Research and Strategy at Open Doors International

Previous books by Kurt Bruner

FATHERLESS

CHILDLESS

GODLESS

FINDING GOD IN *THE LORD OF THE RINGS*

FINDING GOD IN THE LAND OF NARNIA

OPRAH'S JESUS

THE PURPOSE OF PASSION

IT STARTS AT HOME

WHY ISN'T GOD NICE?

TRUSTING HIS AWFUL GOODNESS

Kurt Bruner

MONARCH
BOOKS

Oxford UK, and Grand Rapids, USA

Published by Monarch Books
an imprint of
Lion Hudson plc
Wilkinson House, Jordan Hill Road,
Oxford OX2 8DR, England
Email: monarch@lionhudson.com
www.lionhudson.com/monarch

ISBN 978 0 85721 672 4
e-ISBN 978 0 85721 673 1

First edition 2015

Acknowledgments
Unless otherwise stated Scripture quotations are taken from the Holy Bible, New International Version Anglicised. Copyright © 1979, 1984, 2011 Biblica, formerly International Bible Society. Used by permission of Hodder & Stoughton Ltd, an Hachette UK company. All rights reserved. "NIV" is a registered trademark of Biblica. UK trademark number 1448790.
Extracts marked KJV are taken from The Authorized (King James) Version. Rights in the Authorized Version are vested in the Crown. Reproduced by permission of the Crown's patentee, Cambridge University Press.
Extracts marked NKJV are taken from the New King James Version. Copyright © 1982 by Thomas Nelson, Inc. Used by permission. All right reserved.
Extract pp. 15–16 taken from A Grief Observed by C.S. Lewis, copyright © C.S. Lewis Pte. Ltd. 1961. Extract p. 120 taken from Mere Christianity by C.S Lewis, copyright © C.S. Lewis Pte. Ltd. 1942, 1943, 1944, 1952. Extract p. 128 taken from The Great Divorce by C.S. Lewis, copyright © C.S. Lewis Pte. Ltd. 1946. Extracts reprinted by permission.

A catalogue record for this book is available from the British Library

Printed and bound in the UK, August 2015, LH26

The author is represented by MacGregor Literary, Inc. of Manzanita, OR, U.S.A.

To persecuted believers living where following Jesus costs the most.

Contents

Introduction

An Awful Goodness

What do people mean when they say, "I am not afraid of God because I know He is good?" Have they never been to a dentist?

C. S. Lewis

His name, no kidding, was Doctor Love. Who could fear a man with such an inviting moniker stenciled across his office door? Entering the waiting room as a five-year-old rookie, I assumed Doctor Love would rank among the nicest people I'd ever met; a friendly, kid-loving native of Mr. Roger's neighborhood wearing polyester pants, white laced deck shoes and one of those mid-length, untucked dentist shirts. After a few minutes of chitchat and a casual glance inside my mouth, the exam would conclude with the nice nurse handing me a big red Tootsie Pop sucker.

Parents aren't expected to tell kids the truth about dentists. But I had three older siblings who could have clued me in. But they left me to my delusion—and probably relished my disillusion. I entered the experience overconfident in my preschool teeth-brushing prowess, and under-informed about stainless steel tools designed to torture little mouths – especially that pointy, curved pick used to nip virgin gums while clearing away plaque. And who knew that red Tootsie Pops rot your teeth?

No one ever explained to me that "Love" was our dentist's name, not his job description. Doctor Love was indeed a nice man who liked kids. But his role required doing what I needed but would never request, or want. Which is why dentists make me think of God.

"I could sing of his love forever!" You may recognize the words to the once-popular worship song. Some sang it with lifted hands, others in tearful celebration. I've occasionally wondered why no one has written a second verse to that song, a verse proclaiming "I could sing of his *wrath* forever!" Isn't God as much justice as He is grace? Reading the Scriptures, it seems that God never intended for every snapshot to be taken from His "best" side. When we worship only part of God, we worship a false God. But we seem to prefer the partial phony to the awful reality.

Let's be honest. The Almighty, the One with "Love" stenciled across his heavenly door, seems to do (or at least allow) some pretty dreadful stuff. It's no wonder we sometimes avoid His office, seeing religion as a last resort when aspirin, ice packs and other coping mechanisms fail to get rid of life's toothaches. Even those who do join God's fan club find themselves wondering why their spiritual siblings failed to mention the Lord's less flattering traits. We never seem to get around to that while introducing seekers to the savior our praise choruses portray as a spoonful of sugar. We conveniently skip over the part about medicine going down.

I suppose it has always been like that.

The Israelites sang and danced before Jehovah when He delivered them from slavery. But they jumped ship to a golden calf when times got tough.

Job's wife attended services faithfully with him while the good times rolled. She told her husband to "Curse God and die!" (Job 2:9) when fortunes turned.

The crowds swarmed to Jesus while He healed the sick and fed the hungry. They high-tailed it out of there when He starting talking about eating His flesh and carrying a cross.

Truth is, I probably would have done the same in each of their places. I guess I prefer the phony. Don't we all?

Where was God?

As I write these words, rescue workers are attempting to find survivors and dead bodies scattered throughout neighborhoods overwhelmed by yet another natural disaster. Pick any such tragedy and you'll find the same blank stares of disbelief. On the faces of those in the Philippines struck by Typhoon Haiyan in November of 2013. Or the faces of those hit by Hurricane Katrina eight years before, transforming New Orleans from a thriving cultural center to a death trap literally overnight. Like everyone else, I couldn't stop reading and watching news reports detailing the damage and devastation to thousands of lives. Reporters and politicians pointed fingers, trying to attach blame for poorly orchestrated evacuation and recovery efforts. People wanted to know why the mayor, governor, or president didn't do something sooner. In reality, no government official could have done anything to prevent what was described as the worst natural disaster in our nation's history. The storm hit. The protective levies broke. People died. Survivors lost homes, jobs, and loved ones. Everything else is damage control.

God is the only one who could have prevented the devastation. He knew where and when the storm would hit. He knew sick, elderly widows would be stranded due to inadequate evacuation capacity. He knew little children would be drowned if they couldn't get out of town. Yet He did nothing to stop it.

Now the rest of us are left to care for widows and orphans, feed the hungry, clothe and shelter the homeless. Why, we wonder, didn't He keep them from becoming widows, orphans, hungry, and homeless to begin with? How much effort would it have taken for God, Creator of the universe, to calm the winds like He did to impress the disciples on the Sea of Galilee? Could it be that He actually intended this to happen? Or, perish the thought, caused it?

The same dreadful thoughts cross all of our minds when the "finger of fate" jabs closer to home.

Square peg

During the fifth month, Olivia should feel the baby kicking, should excitedly pull my hand onto her belly while lying in bed so that I can feel it, too. The baby seemed healthy weeks earlier, a strong heartbeat prompting the usual excitement. When that changed we became anxious, called the doctor, and obediently visited the radiology lab. The technician spread the gel and moved the probe around my wife's abdomen, like she did during Kyle and Shaun's stay in the womb. We saw faint images on the screen that looked like a head and an arm, just like before. But this time was different. I noticed the technician staring into the screen and making notes on the page, as if trying to avoid eye contact. She hates this part of her job.

We drove to the doctor's office to learn the results. Only doctors are allowed to deliver bad news. The trip remained quiet, both of us feeling the dread of imminent grief. "I'm sorry about your baby." The doctor's warm, compassionate voice opened the dike of tears. As expected, our baby had died.

The next several hours were among the most difficult of our lives—checking into the hospital, enduring five hours of induced labor, delivering a child who would never breathe. Since in the same hospital we had known the joy of Shaun's birth, the nurses sensitively put us in a room down the hall, away from the maternity ward. The last thing we needed to hear was the happy sound of crying newborns. The hospital reserved our hall for another kind of crying.

I managed to "remain strong" for Olivia until shortly after the baby's birth, or rather, death. Our friends arrived at the hospital with the older boys. Kyle was five, old enough to feel very excited about "baby Todd's" impending arrival, but too young to understand the loss. I had the task of trying to explain to him something I didn't understand myself.

"The baby died," I said through a trembling voice.

Kyle's eyes immediately filled with tears. "Why?" came the question I couldn't answer. Just a few days earlier, Kyle had been making plans to play with his new sibling. Now, he was fumbling to fit the square peg of death into the round hole of life.

I suppose I could have said something about God taking Todd so that He could have another baby in heaven, or that death is just a natural part of life. But I couldn't. Todd had simply died. It happens. And it is sad. So I explained that we had to love on Mommy and cry together, which we did in the quiet hospital wing, now dark with sorrow.

I had encountered death before. Great-grandma Horan died when I was fairly young. But great-grandmas are supposed to die. I lost my Grandma and Grandpa Grey, and Grandma Bruner. Again, we expect death to take the elderly.

It took the death of my best boyhood friend, Don, to make death real to me. He died at age twenty-one in a plane crash. I watched a news report of a crash. Recognized the area as near my childhood home. Never expected to know anyone involved. Got a call a few hours later from a friend saying Don was on that plane. Attended a memorial service without a body to view.

And then there was Cheryl, my thirty-something aunt. She was like a second mom. Cheryl knew the cancer would take her, so asked my wife and me to sing at her funeral. She loved a song titled "Someday we'll never have to say goodbye." But we *were* saying goodbye. We wept more than we sang. Thirty-something is too young to die. So is twenty-one. So is the fifth month.

I know that death will someday strike my home again. It might take other friends, parents, my wife, a son, or daughter.

It will probably come unexpectedly, perhaps cruelly. And no matter how many pep talks I give myself trying to accept death as "natural" I will wonder why a God who claims to love me couldn't invest a few seconds to prevent my pain.

Similarly uncomfortable questions haunt me daily as I observe "acts of God" that appear heartless, even sadistic.

Shortly after the loss of his beloved wife, Joy, C. S. Lewis penned a scandalously honest critique of God. So honest, in fact, it was originally published under another name. *A Grief Observed* chronicles the feelings and reflections of a man who, despite loving the Lord, went through a season in which he didn't like Him much. "Doctor Love" had just put Lewis's bride through the torture of bone cancer before shoving her through death's door.

Lewis describes a silent heaven: a God ready and waiting to celebrate during happy times who seemed to vanish when he needed Him most. Lewis wonders whether human beings are mere rats in a cosmic laboratory. Usually well fed and pampered, we come to view God as the gracious sustainer of life. But the whole time He is actually preparing the next cruel experiment. In the end, Lewis abandons the idea that God is bad, coming to a far worse conclusion.

> *The terrible thing is that a perfectly good God is in this matter hardly less formidable than a Cosmic Sadist. The more we believe that God hurts only to heal, the less we can believe that there is any use in begging for tenderness. A cruel man might be bribed—might grow tired of his*

vile sport—might have a temporary fit of mercy, as
alcoholics have fits of sobriety. But suppose that what you
are up against is a surgeon whose intentions are wholly
good. The kinder and more conscientious he is, the more
inexorably he will go on cutting.[1]

Despite much evidence to the contrary, I believe God to be good. Like C. S. Lewis, and every other person who has ever lived, I also know Him to be awful. This book grows out of a desire to relate to God as He is, rather than as we wish Him to be. Doing so requires confronting some unsettling questions like why a God of love sometimes seems so unloving, even mean. We celebrate a God who is nice, One who rescues, rewards, and redeems. But what about when He deserts, disciplines, and damns? Is God schizophrenic, moving in and out of opposing personalities? One minute, gentle shepherd: the next, angry judge?

Close friends?

Do you remember Jesus' greatest commandment? "Love the Lord your God with all your heart, with all your soul, and with all your mind" (NKJV). Have you ever asked yourself why He had to give such an order? I never "commanded" my wife to love me. She did it of her own free will, supposedly because I'm a lovable guy. Could it be that we are commanded to love God because we don't always consider Him lovable?

I have the honor of serving persecuted believers in my work with Open Doors International. Our work has intensified in recent years due to the spread of Islamic extremism. In a rapidly growing portion of our world, followers of Jesus Christ are, at best, ostracized and, at worst, beheaded or burned alive. But then, the Lord gave us fair warning.

"If they persecuted Me, they will also persecute you." (John 15:20 NKJV)

"They will deliver you up to tribulation and kill you, and you will be hated by all nations for My name's sake." (Matthew 24:9 NKJV)

Like other revolutionaries, the founder of our movement said, "Come, follow me." Unlike the rest, however, He meant an unexpected destination. Instead of fame, power or wealth He offered derision, weakness, and poverty. Rather than the trouble-free good life, He promised the supreme instrument of torture when He said, "If anyone desires to come after Me, let him deny himself, and take up his cross, and follow Me." (Matthew 16:24 NKJV)

The story is told of an ancient saint who suffered a particularly difficult, unspecified trial. She said that the Lord consoled her with the reminder, "This is how I always treat my friends." Her honest reply? "Then, Lord, it is not surprising that You have so few."[2]

God does have a few friends. But they want to skip Good Friday and hurry on to Easter.[3] A God of love who rises from the dead: that makes for a great religion. Why mess it up with talk of suffering and death?

Christianity would look quite different if I were allowed to write its glossary. My version would associate "love" with kind, gentle, patient, accepting, and non-judgmental. I like those words more than words like anger, law, condemnation, and hell. The former conjures images of Mother Teresa caring for the destitute, and soup kitchen volunteers feeding homeless drunks. The latter suggests angry preachers shouting hellfire and brimstone. So I would edit them out.

This book has one simple premise; that a God who is only nice isn't enough. And if we intend to be His friend, we must accept Him as He is.

One who rewards what is right, who must punish what is wrong.

One who extends grace, and upholds justice.

He redeems the lost. But He also thwarts the wicked.

The Scriptures call Jesus Christ "the Lion of Judah" and "the Lamb of God."

One is awful. Both are good.

Each chapter of this book explores how the things we like about God are intimately connected to the things we don't. You don't have time to read and I don't have time to write about every biblical passage that puts a knot in our stomachs. We will only scratch the surface. But we will go far enough to face some of the most challenging questions that emerge when we take seriously the awful goodness God has revealed Himself to be.

1

Perfect Love
Barney Was Wrong

When my older kids were little, they routinely watched a very popular television show starring Barney the Dinosaur. I've never met a parent who liked Barney. My own aversion began when our first child entered those delightful toddler years when new words provide the daily family highlight such as "bubble" or "ball" or, best of all, "daddy." Each day I looked forward to walking into the house to the sounds of my wife's pronouncement, "Daddy's home!" followed by Kyle's little feet running toward the door with arms outstretched for our ritual hug and tickle-fest. It was wonderful.

That is, until *he* entered the picture.

Kyle discovered Barney at about two years old. The PBS program aired during the same thirty-minute timeslot as my homecoming. I will never forget the first time I walked in the door, heard "Daddy's home!" and waited for running feet that never came. Instead, Kyle's eyes remained glued to a hyperactive, purple lizard singing public domain tunes with altered lyrics. Go ahead, tear out my heart!

Almost every kid of the era loved Barney. I suppose that makes sense. After all, from a child's naïve perspective, what's not to like? Where else could you find a costumed grown-up who would dance and sing to you for thirty minutes, closing the experience with those affirming words, "I love you. You love me. We're a happy family." Sure, his voice sounded like a nerd with severe nasal congestion, but a very friendly nerd. And unlike Daddy, Barney never used a stern voice, never said "no," and never slapped your hand when you reached for the stove. Besides, Daddy would still be there to hug after the credits rolled.

I often wonder whether we adults have our own version of Barney. He isn't a big purple dinosaur, but someone we call God. He is not the real God, but the sort we prefer: a God always kind, and who never says no or slaps our hand when we do something wrong. Our view of Him has emerged out of what I call Barney Theology, a religious trend invading every faith tradition. Its one overarching conviction: *God is love*. Certainly, that is a good thing. I like love. I need love. But I need something more than love, as do we all.

During seminary, I had a job answering letters sent to a well-known radio psychologist. Many of the stories described actual childhood experiences worse than my most troubling nightmares. Folks wrote for advice, for comfort, or perhaps just because they needed to tell someone they didn't know personally. I remember one letter from a teen I'll call Alice, whose stepfather sexually abused her with the narrow end of a baseball bat. She described physical pain so intense it made her dizzy to the point of fainting. She described the confusion, wondering what she had done to deserve such abuse. She asked why God didn't stop it from continuing. I had read hundreds of letters describing sexual abuse, but this one boiled my blood like no other. I felt sick to my stomach, wishing I could get my hands on the man who would take a child's innocence in such a cruel and perverted manner.

I sometimes imagine what it must have been like for Alice growing up in such a home. I wonder what thoughts would run through her mind as she sat watching Barney the Dinosaur sing his closing song: "I love you. You love me. We're a happy family." Would she feel affirmed with such a warm, verbal hug? Would she hear a message of happiness to help ease her pain? I doubt it. She would probably see right through its empty simplicity. She might laugh in scornful despair. Perhaps spit at the television screen. You see, that young girl knows that no song in the universe, regardless of how kind and affirming, can rescue her from the torture she endures, or the hate it inflames.

I wonder how Alice would feel sitting in a modern worship service, perhaps in one of our shopping-mall-sized evangelical congregations bustling with activity. You know the type: multiple services, coffee bar, bookstore, and a friendly yet efficient parking crew. Inside the service, thousands gather to participate in collective praise led by a cutting-edge band and large screen projection. Everything is done with excellence, like well-produced television. Hands are raised. Faces smile. Tears flow. Beautiful melodies and energetic rhythms stir the soul. They celebrate a nice God, a God who loves everyone, forgives everything—more friend and lover than judge and jury.

But Alice doesn't relate. She doesn't discount the experience of those around her. It just doesn't connect to her own. The worship seems Pollyanna-ish, songs of those glad for their happiness rather than desperate in their pain. Sure, it is nice to know God loves her in the midst of her abuse. But then, so does Barney.

Perhaps Alice leaves church and stops by her local bookstore. After grabbing a latte from the adjoining coffee shop, she takes a moment to scan the religious section. The title of a little book by Rabbi Harold Kushner grabs her attention, *When Bad Things Happen to Good People*. Kushner knows pain, not only because he ministers to many hurting people, but because his own precious son suffered and died from a rare disease that prevented proper growth and forced premature aging. Reading the tale of a little boy suffering while his helpless parents watch convinces Alice that Kushner has honestly confronted a cruel world. He might have answers for her. He focuses on the book of Job. The story of a man who, like Kushner himself, suffered great loss and pain while his "Why?" seemed to bounce off heaven's door. She flips to the conclusion to see what answers she might find.

> *Are you capable of forgiving and loving God even when you have found out that He is not perfect, even when He has let you down and disappointed you by permitting bad luck and sickness and cruelty in His world, and permitting some of those things to happen to you? Can you learn to love and forgive Him despite His limitations,*

as Job does, and as you once learned to forgive and
love your parents even though they were not as wise, as
strong, or as perfect as you needed them to be?[4]

Kushner's God seems a kindly grandfather, cringing at the bad things happening to His beloved children. Forced to choose between an all-powerful God who allows suffering and an all-loving God with limited power, Kushner chooses the latter. His God seems feeble. He wants to stop our pain, but the bully of evil is younger and stronger. So God offers the only thing He can: consolation, sympathy, love.

Nice, Alice reflects, *but not enough.*

After placing Kushner's book back on the shelf, Alice continues her search. She spots another best-seller: Neale Donald Walsch's *Conversations With God*. With millions of readers, she supposes, the author must offer something that can help her. Walsch says he has questioned God directly about life, and recorded the responses. Maybe his more eastern, pantheistic answers will provide what Alice needs. Thumbing through the book, she discovers a God even nicer than the one of Christians and Jews. He doesn't judge anyone for anything, and He asks Alice to go and do likewise.

In the largest sense, all the "bad" things that happen are
of your choosing. The mistake is not in choosing them,
but in calling them bad…

Evil is that which you call evil. Yet even that I love
… I do not love hot more than cold, high more than low,
left more than right. It is all relative. It is all part of what

> *is … I do not love "good" more than I love "bad." Hitler*
> *went to heaven. When you understand this, you will*
> *understand God.*[5]

So, the problem is not what Alice suffers, but how Alice perceives the suffering. What she calls bad is part of what God loves. If Hitler went to heaven, then who is she to hold a grudge against her abuser? After all, God loves everyone. In the words of Barney, "We're a happy family."

None of these happy, friendly, non-judgmental images of God can satisfy Alice. Her heart cries out for a God who gets angry at evil and does something about it. Alice wants… no, Alice *deserves* more.

Barney Theology turns the once-grand contribution of religion into little more than a frail playground monitor pleading with earth's cruel bullies, "Please be nice." But what about when they aren't nice? Our deepest feelings abandon the God we thought we preferred.

If we get honest with ourselves, we don't want Hitler going to heaven. We want him judged for his crimes against humanity.

We don't want a child suffering because God can do nothing to stop it. We want to believe that even the bad can be used for some greater purpose, and that there will be eventual restoration.

We don't want Alice's abuser enjoying with impunity her perverse tortures. We want him punished.

"It will not do to merely overlook the wrong," wrote Richard John Neuhaus. "We could not bear to live in a world where wrong is taken lightly, where right and wrong finally make no difference."[6]

God doesn't forgive us because evil is no big deal. He forgives us because He took it seriously enough to do something about it.

No matter how many Barney songs I sing about a God of love, my heart knows that the wrong in our world needs to be set right: something that will happen only when the One we want to see as nonjudgmental finally acts to condemn evil and its perpetrators.

On one hand, I don't want to believe in hell. On the other, I hope with all my being that it exists. You see, I want a God who is more than love. I want a God who is justice. A God who sets things right and punishes evil.

Like Alice, I want him to do it *now*. But I'll take it someday.

GOING DEEPER

Use the following to prompt further reflection, or to facilitate a group discussion.

Exodus 20:5–6 says, "For I, the Lord your God, am a jealous God, visiting the iniquity of the fathers on the children to the third and fourth generations of those who hate Me, but showing mercy to thousands, to those who love Me and keep My commandments" (NKJV).

- Does allowing the consequences of one's parents' and grandparents' sin to affect someone's life seem nice, or mean?

- We know that the Bible contains hyperbole statements that exaggerate to emphasize a true principle. Since the children of abusers and addicts suffer the fallout of their parents' sin, does this statement ring true to what we observe in our fallen world?

- Is it possible this statement is actually a statement of hope rather than judgment since it implies "thousands" receive mercy while only a few generations feel the impact of sin?

Romans 5:8 says that "God demonstrates His own love toward us, in that while we were still sinners, Christ died for us" (NKJV) while John 3:16 tells us that "God so loved the world that He gave His only begotten Son, that whoever believes in Him should not perish but have everlasting life."

- These scriptures suggest that God initiated our salvation "while we were still sinners" yet leaves the decision of whether or not to receive salvation in our court. How might this same freedom to choose influence the reality of human evil in our world?

- Clearly God intervenes in human affairs when it comes to redeeming sin. Why doesn't He seem to intervene when it comes to preventing it?

- Would taking away our freedom to choose evil also undermine our freedom to choose salvation? Why or why not?

2

Strict Father
What Parents Know

Early morning on 25 July 1990, I took my first sip of a drink that tastes like God. Life changed forever when our nine-pound, blood-drenched screaming son Kyle was born.

It happened again two, seven, and ten years later when Shaun, Troy, and Nicole came along. Now I spend my days gulping the good and the bad of what it means to be somebody's daddy, to be their highest earthly representation of a heavenly person. I became and am becoming something God has always been: a father.

While I don't do the job nearly as well, I can relate to how God must feel as the One millions call "Our heavenly Father." My wife shares the feeling, though in very different ways. If I represent God's stability, provision, and strength, Olivia shows His compassion, beauty, and tender caring. Together we give our children a small taste of who He must be. We also share the moments that tell us something of how He must feel, snapshots embedded in the heart's photo album.

Click—I recall the flutter of life as my hand rests on Olivia's protruding belly and the flutter of awe at the knowledge that another human being, my child, would soon journey down the birth canal into a new world.

Click—I recall staring into each tiny infant face mere minutes, hours, and days after they'd been scrunched within the tiny space of Mommy's womb. Miniature eyelashes, ears, and lips. Perfectly formed hands wrapped around my now giant index finger.

Click—I recall hour after hour coaching that first word until finally "Dada" came out (sort of). No one else heard it and it could just as easily have been any word in the dictionary. But it sounded close enough to give my life meaning.

Click—Cheering first steps into Mommy's arms.

Click—Wiping first tumble-down-the-stairs tears.

Click, click, click—Accepting that first open-mouthed, runny nose-laced kiss, then wiping my face before getting two more.

Some of the most awe-inspiring moments come when I clearly see myself in one of our kids. Sometimes too clearly, like the time our oldest embarrassed his fifth-grade teacher by correcting her in front of the class. Totally inappropriate. Entirely out of line. But exactly the kind of thing I would have done at his age. Like his daddy, he has a hard time letting an error go uncorrected. "You know, he takes after you in that way," my wife points out the painfully obvious.

I could do the same. Our second child reflects many of the strengths and weaknesses found in his mother. I see Olivia in Shaun just as clearly as she sees me in Kyle. Even more amazingly, we both see traces of ourselves in all of our kids. From the shape of a nose to the tone of a voice, each expresses our personhood in big and small ways. It is like an artist seeing a bit of himself in what he creates. The painting is wholly other, yet clearly from himself.

I think God allows us to become parents so that we can sample what it feels like for Him to be our father. He must feel about us the way I do my children. While wholly other, I am clearly from Him. I can't help the love I feel for my children, like an irresistible impulse woven into the fabric of my being. So God must love His children. He can't help it.

When she turned one and a half, Nicole reached that phase when children get a kick out of identifying facial features. As with all children, she first mastered the nose. "Where's your nose?" I asked, eager for my budding genius to point to the center of her face. Then came the really good part. She turned her finger around, pointed to my giant beak and struggled to pronounce one of only twenty words in her developing vocabulary: "Nose." We then moved on to other parts: eye, ear, cheek, hair. When we hit the chin, her tiny hand gently cupped itself under my jawbone as my heart melted dead away. Her determined tenderness told me the world and the people around her, the things we adults take for granted, are a marvel. Every new discovery became part of the adventure called learning. I loved cultivating and watching the process. I loved the sense of awe it reawakened in me.

I wonder: does God's heart melt when I reach for His face, or when I struggle to put my discovery into words?

When my boys reached that awkward stage between childhood and puberty, I felt unsure whether to lovingly hug them goodnight or give them a fierce punch in the arm. It was also that stage when I found myself amazed at who they were becoming. Shaun was the imaginative dreamer and artist. His mind overflowed with possibilities that he would reflect on the page. He would hand me his latest creation, eager for my approval. "Good job, buddy!" An inadequate expression of how I really felt. He did with pencil and crayon what I do with words—making something out of nothing. The best ones ended up in our collection of imperfect masterpieces.

Troy proved to be a gifted musician. I quit piano lessons long before reaching his current skill level on the keyboard. He can also play the drums and guitar. As I watch him play with the church worship band, I can't believe my child has mastered such difficult music. "That was great! I'm proud of you." Equally inadequate. But I really am.

I wonder: does God's heart thrill when I mimic His ability to create something out of nothing? Does He get a lump in his throat when I use the talents He gave?

Of course, for every moment of parental pride, joy or awe, there has been a moment of frustration, conflict, and heartache. They all come as a package. Our home has seen more than its share of irresponsible spills, nap-deprived tantrums, and willfully defiant rebellion. As the father, I routinely have to play the role of disciplinarian. I now hear my own father's words coming out of my mouth.

"Don't speak to your mother like that!"

"Go to your room and wait for me."

"You have three seconds to change that attitude!"

I don't like being stern. But it is a necessary part of the job. I love my children too much to overlook wrong behavior. Still, it can be painful. No matter how many times I correct the kids, another round of conflict always looms on the horizon. You have to develop thick skin as the father of young children. Being respectful doesn't come any more naturally for them than it did for you or me. It has to be learned. It has to be taught.

I wonder: does our heavenly Father tire of our bad attitudes? Does He find it necessary to be stern at times, loving us too much to overlook wrong?

Every day I take another gulp of what God must feel. I can't help loving my kids, imperfections and all. I would die for them. I suppose He would, too.

Our Father

When the disciples asked Jesus to teach them how to pray, He gave them a prototype. His words have become familiar to the religiously devout or to anyone forced to attend church as a child. Recall sixty-six of the most famous words Jesus ever spoke.

Our Father in heaven, Hallowed be Your name. Your kingdom come. Your will be done On earth, as it is in heaven. Give us this day our daily bread. And forgive us our debts, as we forgive our debtors. And do not lead us into temptation, But deliver us from the evil one.

For Yours is the kingdom and the power and the glory
forever. Amen.[7]

Millions of people recite those words every Sunday. But how many grasp the profound nature of the first two? Jesus invites us to call God "Our Father." He taught us that God cares about the details of his children's lives: concerns Himself with our daily provision and with our right behavior. But then, what good father doesn't?

The title "Father" should prompt wonderful memories of happy childhood days under the firm, loving protection of paternal care. Sadly, for some, the title can dredge up painful feelings of a dad who seemed always angry, self-consumed, or absent. But we all recognize a good dad when we see one.

It is one thing to view God as a father. It is quite another thing to see God through the eyes of one who has been a father. I know what it is to see myself in my children and to derive my joy from their happiness. I know what it is to want to protect them from harm, yet realize that I must let them make and learn from their own mistakes. I know what it is to become angry at their disobedience while hating the need to punish. I know what it is to lay aside my own desires and dreams in order to meet the needs of my child.

In short, I know something of how God must feel, because He has allowed me a small taste by making me somebody's daddy. And of the many things being a father has taught me about Him, I am most certain of this one thing. God can't help loving us.

Many of us grew up hearing stories from both the Old Testament and New Testament Scriptures. And some of us received the mistaken impression that there are two different Gods. The Old Testament depicts a demanding deity who exacts judgment on those who cross the line. The New Testament, by contrast, presents the nicer version named Jesus. He would never do some of those nasty things attributed to the other God. If only Jesus had been around, the Old Testament would have been a much more pleasant book.

Jesus wouldn't have caused a flood to drown most of humanity, not to mention innocent little puppies and fluffy bunny rabbits.

Jesus wouldn't have sent ten plagues on the Egyptians. Or at least, He wouldn't have sent lice, flies, and locusts, knowing how much people hate bugs.

Jesus wouldn't have let Job suffer or lose his children. And He would have given him a more supportive wife.

After all, unlike the Old Testament version of God, Jesus loved people.

Nineteenth-century pastor and writer George MacDonald grappled with seemingly contradictory portrayals of God's character. He said, "I love the one God seen in the face of Jesus Christ."[8] That's why he criticized Christian ministers who described us as sinners in the hands of an angry God. MacDonald agreed that we are sinners. He also agreed that God hates sin. But he rejected the notion that God's hatred spilled over onto His children. Every parent hates childhood diseases. But they don't spank their kids for getting a fever.

George MacDonald's sermon titled *Justice* reminds us that the God of both the Old and New Testament is, first and foremost, a father.

> *In God shall we imagine a distinction of office and*
> *character? God is one; and the depth of foolishness is*
> *reached by that theology which talks of God as if he held*
> *different offices, and differed in each ... It represents him,*
> *for instance, as having to do that as a magistrate which*
> *as a father he would not do!*[9]

Jesus didn't teach us to pray "Our Father in heaven" as a public relations stunt, as if to attach a friendlier label to someone harsh and demanding. He was reminding us of a reality that had been obscured by religious legalism.

MacDonald goes on. "They think of the father of souls as if he had abdicated his fatherhood for their sins, and assumed the judge ... If he put off his fatherhood ... he puts off with it all relation to us."[10]

In short, God can only relate to us as a father because that's who He is.

So why so many laws, warnings, and acts of judgment?

Because, says MacDonald, "The eternal love will not be moved to yield you to the selfishness that is killing you."[11]

Every one of us contracted a childhood disease called sin. Our hot foreheads betray self-centered and self-destructive propensities that no loving father would leave untreated.

On trial

When my older children were about ages nine, seven and two, I planned an activity that drove home the truth MacDonald was trying to express.

The boys looked forward to our weekly family night routine when Olivia and I invested thirty minutes having fun with the kids in a way that opened the door for faith conversations. Typical family night activities included blowing up balloons to discuss how, just like air, God is real even though we can't see Him; or the time we gave them each a tube of toothpaste to see who could empty it the fastest right before offering $20 to the one who could put the paste back in the tube. Like the toothpaste, we can't take back words once they leave our mouths. As you might imagine, the boys had come to expect fun and laughter rather than what they would experience on this particular evening.

"We are going to trial!" I announced when they asked what activity we had planned for family night. "Go in the next room with Bailiff Mom. She will explain proper courtroom etiquette while I put on my judge's gown."

A few minutes later, they found me in my home office wearing a blanket over my shoulders. I sat at my desk facing three empty chairs.

"All rise," I announced for effect, even though they were already standing. "This is the case of Bruner versus Bruner, Bruner, and Bruner! Let the accused take their seats."

Accused? they wondered. *Of what?*

They had been set up the prior family night when we discussed *the law of love.* I recall them nodding heads in agreement when we explained that we demonstrate our love through obedience based upon Jesus' words in John 14:15. We created a list of how they could demonstrate such love: obeying Mommy without arguing, doing their chores without complaining, etc.

"You've been accused of violating the law of love," I explained. "How do you plead?"

Kyle, the eldest, spoke first. "Not guilty!"

"Not guilty?" I shouted. "Are you sure you want to enter a plea of not guilty? You see, Mom is both the bailiff and the chief witness in this case."

He appeared nervous, but held firm. "Not guilty."

"I'm guilty," said seven-year-old Shaun. He was probably hoping for a deal.

Troy was too young to understand what was happening, just happy to be part of the experience.

"I have in my possession a copy of a list we created last week with your signatures indicating you had agreed to obey the law of love for one full week. I now call Mom to testify as to whether or not you kept that promise."

Needless to say, all three boys stood condemned within a few minutes. I took up a toy judge's mallet in my hand and banged it on the desktop. "I hereby declare all three of you guilty. Your sentence is to receive paddle swats on the bottom until pain. Bend over your chairs!"

Eyes opened wide.

"Come on, Dad!" came the objections. "This is family night. It's supposed to be fun."

"Are you guilty of the crime?" I asked.

"Well, yes," they agreed.

"You knew what you did was wrong?"

Sheepish nods.

"And you did it anyway?"

"Well, yes, but…"

"Then you're guilty without excuse. Assume the spanking position now."

That's when Olivia pulled out a large swatting paddle, the kind used in schools back in the Dark Ages.

The boys didn't know what to think or what to do. Was this a fun activity, or a discipline session? Was Mom really going to swat them with that giant plank of wood?

Olivia approached Kyle while raising the paddle. The boys suddenly realized this was no joke: that she fully intended to carry out the sentence. They began to quiver at the anticipation of a swooshing sound followed by a painful smack on the rear end.

"Wait a second!" I said, just before Olivia swung the paddle.

I stood up. "I'm your judge," I said while laying down the mallet. "But I'm also your father. I love you, and I don't want to see you suffer."

They breathed a sigh of relief as I removed the blanket from my shoulders.

"But someone needs to take the punishment for what you've done. So I will."

A different expression came over each of the boys' faces. They didn't want to get swatted, but they knew I didn't deserve it either.

I moved to the chair and bent over. Olivia got a big grin on her face. Then she let me have it.

We all moved into the living room to talk about the activity.

"What just happened?" I asked the boys.

Shaun spoke first. "That was just like Jesus!"

Point made and received.

God is a righteous, holy judge. In His presence we know ourselves unclean. We see our guilt over breaking the very commandments we know are best for us.

But God is also our father. He knows our weaknesses. He took the consequences of sin upon Himself, thus preserving justice while demonstrating love.

That day our family experienced a small taste of a God who is both a strict judge and a loving father.

GOING DEEPER

Use the following to prompt further reflection, or to facilitate a group discussion.

In Matthew 6:9 Jesus invites his disciples to call God "Our Father in heaven" rather than the common expression "God of our fathers."

- What does the title "Our Father" suggest about how God wants us to relate to Him?

- In what ways does this influence the common perception of God as Creator and/or law-giver?

The apostle Paul adopted this same title when he wrote to early Christians. (See Romans 1:7, 1 Corinthians 1:3, Galatians 1:4, Ephesians 1:2, Philippians 1:2, Colossians 1:2, 1 Thessalonians 1:1, 1 Timothy 1:2, Titus 1:4, Philemon 1:3.)

- How might the phrase "God our Father" have impacted early believers who had been raised to worship pagan and mythic deities such as Zeus and Apollo?

- If you are a parent, identify some ways your view of God might differ from those who have never experienced fatherhood or motherhood.

3

Divine Comedian

God Laughs with Us, Not at Us

I remember the first time I saw a Christian fish logo on the back of a car. Impressed by the connection to the secret symbol of the early church, I thought, *Now, that's cool.*

Years later, I saw the same logo with feet on the bottom and the name "Darwin" in the middle. Struck by the clever irony, I remember thinking, *Now, that's funny!*

I suppose I should have felt offended rather than tickled. Someone, somewhere created that logo in an effort to slam Christians against the glass: a person who probably takes his or her unbelief way too seriously. I'm sure my laughing missed the intent.

But other believers felt the insult, even going so far as to launch a counterattack on their bumpers by displaying a reduced Darwin fish being eaten by a larger Christian fish in "survival of the fittest" manner. Not quite as original, kind of like kids shouting, "Same to you and more of it!" But a worthy effort, nonetheless.

Do you remember the awkward thrill of that first dirty word uttered with your grade-school friends? Knowing it was wrong made it worth doing. The risk of being caught made it exciting. Both prompted nervous laughter.

Satire, unlike other forms of heckling, has such an effect because it doesn't play fair. It creates an exaggerated caricature that misrepresents or overstates. When debating, both sides must receive equal time and voice. In satire, one side has a good snicker at the other's expense. Sometimes, it is a nervous laugh such as in Monty Python's 1979 release, *Life of Brian*.

The film opens with a musical score reminiscent of biblical epics such as *Ben Hur* or *King of Kings*, angelic voices serenading the silhouette of three camel-riding wise men following a star into the city of Bethlehem. They find a stable with a young mother whose infant child lies in a straw-filled manger among the animals. As they attempt to offer gifts of gold, frankincense, and myrrh, the wise men get verbally accosted by the woman they have frightened with their annoying intrusion. It is not the blessed virgin, mother of Jesus, the holy Son of God. It is squealing Monty Python star Terry Jones, portraying a promiscuous woman, mother of Brian the bastard son of a Roman guard. Quickly realizing their mistake, the wise men retrieve their gifts and scurry off to worship the true object of their quest, just next door.

Born on the same day in the next stable, the rest of Brian's life similarly parallels that of Jesus, including some fringe encounters between the two. One of the funniest scenes has Brian and others listening to Jesus' famous Sermon on the Mount from the back of the crowd. But they are so far away they strain to hear properly.

"Speak up!" shouts Brian's agitated mother. "I can't hear a thing!"

Neither, it seems, can the others.

"What was that?" asks a nobleman who didn't quite catch Jesus' last phrase.

"I think it was, 'Blessed are the cheese makers,'" offers a fellow bystander.

"What's so special about cheese makers?" someone asks with a sigh.

"Well, obviously it's not meant to be taken literally," responds the nobleman in smug confidence of his interpretative skills. "It refers to any manufacturer of dairy products."

Similar misunderstandings and misinterpretations abound, including the assumption that some Greek is going to inherit the earth. "Did anyone catch his name?" asks one hoping to join the windfall.

In another scene, Brian encounters an unusual beggar. Perfectly healthy, he sits on the side of the road with cup extended, shouting, "Alms for an ex-leper?" Upon inquiry, Brian learns that the man was a victim of Jesus' healing powers.

"One minute I'm a leper with a trade, the next minute my livelihood is gone. Bloody do-gooder!" sneers the healed man. Apparently, miracles mess up the way things are meant to be. People should leave well enough alone.

Later, while running from authorities who want him arrested for involvement with a group of incompetent insurgents, Brian finds himself in a tight spot. He pretends to be a traveling preacher. A small crowd gathers to listen, but Brian loses his train of thought in mid-sentence.

"To them only shall be given…"

"Shall be given what?" asks the crowd.

"Oh, nothing." An honest reply, but not good enough for his self-appointed disciples. So they fill in the blanks, each presumption building on the last.

"It must be a secret."

"What is the secret?"

"What is the secret of eternal life?"

"I want to know the secret of eternal life!"

"Tell us, master!"

Before he knows what has happened, a crowd follows Brian, clinging to (though misunderstanding) his every word and cradling his dropped sandal as a religious relic. He attempts to correct their impressions, but can't dissuade their erroneous speculation about his mission and the meaning of his "example."

While hiding from the crowd in hopes of fleeing their adoration, Brian steps on the foot of an old hermit who has maintained a vow of strict silence for eighteen years, causing the man to scream in pain. When the crowd learns that Brian has "healed" one who had been speechless, it only fuels their zealous conjecture that he is the true Messiah.

"I'm not the Messiah!" insists an exasperated Brian.

"I say you are, Lord," retorts one disciple. "And I should know. I've followed a few."

In the end, Brian finds himself dying on a cross as part of a group crucifixion. His fellow conspirators pay their respects by reading a formal referendum honoring Brian for staying true to the point of martyrdom. They even sing him a robust round of "For he's a jolly good fellow!" in celebration of his sacrificial example for the cause.

Film credits roll as a joyful, ever-optimistic chap hanging alongside Brian encourages him to cheer up and find the silver lining of the situation. He even leads the choir of condemned men in a whistling, pick-me-up tune called, "Always look on the bright side of life."

Life of Brian has much of the nonsensical silliness and irreverent dialogue made legendary by the Monty Python team. But something deeper is at work in its creative choices. The movie consistently hints at the discredited yet lingering arguments against Christ's divinity, portraying Brian as one who could just as easily have been assumed the Messiah by the uneducated, overly eager peasants of his day. Anyone who has studied the standard explanations of liberal theologians will recognize the themes…

- Jesus was the illegitimate son of a Roman guard.

- Jesus did not perform miracles; that would mess up the God-ordained order of things. His followers saw what they wanted to see.

- Jesus was a good teacher, but He never claimed to be Messiah. Disciples read that idea into His words, hearing what they wanted to hear.

- Jesus' crucifixion was not part of some divine plan to save mankind, but an injustice orchestrated by those whose power structure was threatened by His popularity.

- Jesus did not rise from the dead. His disciples stole the body in order to put a happy face on an otherwise tragic ending.

Is *Life of Brian* a funny movie? At times. Is it innocent fun? I don't think so. It is at best a commentary on just how naïve and fanatical man can be when it comes to religious faith. It is at worst a direct slam against the divinity of Christ. Either way, I place its humor in the category of laughter that must have accompanied creating Darwin fish logos and other sacrilegious satire. The kind of laughter evident in the comedy of Hollywood icon Woody Allen.

Nervous laughter

I consider the life of actor, writer, and director Woody Allen irrefutable proof that God has a sense of humor. If his deer in the headlights, horn-rimmed glasses eyes, and paranoid pipsqueak demeanor don't cause one to laugh, his brilliant screenplays will. And I do mean brilliant. Allen has to be one of the sharpest minds ever to bring comedy to the silver screen.

From his Academy Award-winning *Annie Hall*, to the futuristic satire *Sleeper*, to his parody of Dostoevsky's *Crime and Punishment*, Allen has demonstrated an uncanny capacity for finding humor in the most unlikely places. Not the shallow, slapstick humor of most Hollywood fare, but a dark, nihilistic humor of one tormented by the inability to believe.

I will never forget the first time I saw one of Allen's lesser-known, lesser-understood films, titled *Love and Death*—a faint reflection of Tolstoy's classic *War and Peace*. Other than that Allen plays a Russian farmer caught up in the dramatic events of Napoleon's Europe, the two tales bear little resemblance. Allen plays Boris Grushenko, a cowardly embarrassment to his family. But a man in love with his beautiful cousin, Sonya, played by Allen's frequent sidekick, Diane Keaton.

In an opening scene, Boris and Sonya have a remarkably profound conversation for what many might consider a simple comedy, a conversation that reveals Allen's depth as a writer.[12]

Sonja: "Boris, look at this leaf. Isn't it perfect? Ah yes. I definitely think that this is the best of all possible worlds."

Boris shrugs in disinterest, and makes a wisecrack about it being the most expensive world.

Sonja: "Isn't nature incredible!"

Boris: "To me nature is spiders and bugs and big fish eating little fish, and animals eating other animals. It's like an enormous restaurant. That's the way I see it."

Sonja: "Yes, but if God created it, it has to be beautiful, even if His plan's not apparent to us at the moment."

With a roll of his eyes, Boris reveals impatient contempt with the silly beliefs of his lovely, if unsophisticated, cousin.

Boris: "Sonja, what if there is no God?"

Sonja responds in shocked indignation as Boris continues.

Boris: "What if we're just a bunch of absurd people who are running around with no rhyme or reason?"

Sonja: "But if there is no God, then life has no meaning. Why go on living? Why not just commit suicide?"

Boris: "Well, let's not get hysterical! I could be wrong. I'd hate to blow my brains out and then read in the papers they found something."

Nervous laugh number one. Suddenly, the seemingly naïve Sonja becomes an intellectual force to reckon with as the two trade philosophical arguments for and against God.

Sonja: "Boris, let me show you how absurd your position is. Let's say that there is no God and each man is free to do exactly as he chooses. Well, what prevents you from murdering someone?"

Boris: "Murder is immoral."

Sonja: "Immorality is subjective."

Boris: "Yes, but subjectivity is objective."

Sonja: "Not in any rational scheme of perception."

Boris: "Perception is irrational. It implies immanence."

Sonja: "But judgment of any system or a priori relation of phenomena exists in any rational or metaphysical or at least epistemological contradiction to an abstract or an empirical concept such as 'being' or 'to be' or 'to occur in the thing itself' or 'of the thing itself.'"

Boris: Yeah, I've said that many times.

Even those who don't "get the joke" buried in such lofty language, sense nervous laugh number two. When pushed to the wall with real arguments for the existence of an ultimate reality called God, Allen's character has but one response: a well-timed wisecrack.

Sonja: "We must believe in God."

Boris: "If I could just see one miracle—a burning bush, or the seas part, or my Uncle Sasha pick up a check!"

And with that, the conversation ends. But not before revealing an undercurrent of nihilistic angst that has surfaced throughout Woody Allen's creative career. The question of God's existence finds its way into most of Allen's films, and the answer is generally accompanied by the kind of paranoid humor we've come to associate with Allen. Here are a few such gems...

From *Stardust Memories*...

To you—to you I'm an atheist... to God I'm the loyal opposition.

From *Monologue*...

I was in love my freshman year but I did not marry the first girl I fell in love with because there was a tremendous religious conflict at the time. She was an atheist and I was an agnostic. We didn't know which religion not to bring the children up in.

From *Broadway Danny Rose*...

Danny: It's very important to be guilty. I'm guilty all the time and I never did anything. You know? My rabbi, Rabbi Perlstein, used to say we're all guilty in the eyes of God.

Tina: You believe in God?

Danny: No, no. But, uh, I'm guilty over it.

And one of my favorites, from *Crimes and Misdemeanors*…

*My father takes after his Aunt May. She rejected
the Bible because it had an unbelievable central
character.*[13]

What I find most interesting about Woody Allen is his grasp of
the arguments for belief. At times he seems more familiar with
Jewish and Christian theology than many die-hard believers.
How else could he write screenplays in which characters argue
both sides of the God debate? And yet, despite brief beams
of light that a good sense of humor can't help but reflect, his
works possess an omnipresent shadow of despair. So we laugh,
but nervously.

A good laugh

My three sons sit in the back seat as I drive. It is boys' night
out—and Dad is taking them to their favorite fast-food
restaurant. With a wad of cash in my pocket, the fun account
looks full and ready to draw down.

"Do I have to order a kid's meal?" asks Kyle, my eldest,
skinny as a rail despite eating like a rhino. "Or can I get a double
cheeseburger?"

Why not? I figure we can live on the wild side, for once.

"Sortney!" I say in my best Curly voice from the Three Stooges. (Translated: "Certainly," for the uninitiated.) Having amused myself with such a believable impersonation, I go even further, mimicking the high-pitched, prolonged falsetto sound—"wubububbub"—Curly made whenever fleeing a scene. (Translated: "Let's get outta here!") On a roll, I put the icing on the cake by squeezing a pronounced "Nyuk, nyuk, nyuk!" out one side of my mouth. (No English equivalent available.)

Chuckling at myself, I peer through the rear-view mirror to catch a glimpse of what I expect to be laughing children, justifiably proud of their comedic father. "You're the greatest, Dad! No one can do the Three Stooges like you!"

That's what I expect to hear. Instead, I see blank stares. Actually, embarrassed stares. Finally, Kyle speaks. "Um, Dad—what are you doing?"

At that moment, I realized that I had failed my children. Somehow, my boys had lived on this earth for nearly a decade without experiencing the infamous Three Stooges, the greatest guy humor act in human history.

"Do you mean to tell me you've never seen the Three Stooges?" I ask, dumbfounded.

"The three *what*?" asks Shaun, my second born (second deprived boy).

"Oh my goodness!" I scream, the solution already forming in my mind. "Boys, right after we eat, I am taking you to Blockbuster Video."

And so I did. I rented several Three Stooges tapes and rushed home to introduce my sons to Larry, Moe, Curly, Shemp, and Joe. I took time to explain each character, the main plot line of every episode (which took all of ten seconds), and that all true Stooge fans recognize Curly as the best of the bunch.

My wife Olivia watched in perplexed horror. Moms have never understood what guys see in the Stooges. She worried that her kind-hearted angels would start thumping one another on the head and poking each other's eyes. I calmed her fears, explaining that no boy should grow up without the enrichment of Stooge humor—and that I would instruct our sons in the strict safety rules of Stooge imitation. She just shook her head and walked out of the room.

Over the coming months, I introduced my boys to several other great acts, including Abbott and Costello, the Marx Brothers, *The Little Rascals*, and of course, *Gilligan's Island*. Before you knew it, I could imitate almost any great comedic act while driving, and my boys could immediately recognize the source. I had restored my good dad status!

Be it slapstick like the Stooges, or a slightly more sophisticated sitcom like *Seinfeld*, humor is a wonderful gift. And whether prompted by a stand-up comedian or a child's misspeak, laughter feels good.

I figure God must have a wonderful sense of humor. After all, He could have made passing gas an entirely silent activity. Instead, He set up every dad, uncle, and grandpa for the "pull my finger" trick, prompting childhood giggles since the beginning of time.

My Grandpa Grey loved a good laugh. A retired truck driver, he had a rough look with a gentle temperament—kind of a cross between John Wayne and Jimmy Stewart. He and Grandma lived in a small house about a mile from ours. I remember riding my bike to their place nearly every day one summer in order to help Grandpa work on lawnmowers, something he did in retirement to earn extra cash. I was only about ten years old, so I probably got more in the way than anything. Still, I felt like I was doing something.

One day, Grandpa's mischievous side got the best of him—and me. For some reason, he needed to shorten a particular bolt to better fit the mower he was fixing. So, using his hacksaw, Grandpa cut it down to size. I watched as the friction of metal on metal cut through and eventually released the quarter inch of excess bolt, causing it to fall to the ground. "Quick, hand me that piece," ordered Grandpa.

Naïve to the dynamics of metal friction, I dutifully obeyed, glad to finally be of some use. A split second later, I felt the smart of burning flesh, threw the hot metal piece up in the air and yelled out in pain. Just as quickly, I tried to regain my composure as if it had been no big deal, hoping to preserve my façade of manhood.

Nearly forty years later, I can still hear my late grandpa's uncontrolled laughter. The wheezing chuckle lasted for some time in his smoker's throat, and would start all over again when he relayed the story to Grandma and my parents. Admittedly, at first I didn't think it was funny. But it is now one of my favorite

Grandpa Grey memories, one that prompts an occasional chuckle of my own.

What made that moment so funny? How did burning a kid's hand prompt laughter rather than outrage? Why do I look back at the incident with fond rather than angry recollection? I believe it has something to do with the nature of humor, and the deep well of joy it taps.

Laughter is a funny thing. It catches us by surprise, sneaks up and overtakes our composure when we most want it maintained. Have you ever tried to suppress a laugh in church when something strikes your fancy? It can't be done without severe damage to vital internal organs. Or how about the time you found yourself in the middle of a big marital spat, determined not to back down first. Suddenly, for some strange reason, your funny bone got tickled. An odd comment or look made the entire battle seem silly. You reluctantly giggled, making your spouse laugh, too. The tension dissipated, and before you knew it, you were making passionate love to one another. The moment, and maybe the marriage, was saved.

Great comedy is mysteriously wed to surprise. Someone does the unexpected and it makes you laugh. It may be Moe thumping Curly on the head, Robin Williams acting nutty in a most inappropriate setting, or an unsuspecting child eagerly retrieving a hot bolt. It could be the sudden rush of happiness that comes when all hope seems lost, but surprise overtakes the moment. Do you remember the scene in *The Sound of Music* when pursuing Nazis find it impossible to start their cars, even as two nuns confess to their Mother Superior the sin of stealing engine parts? Their unexpected action saves the day—so we laugh, both at the humor of the moment and the relieved assurance that our heroes will indeed escape. The surprise of both prompts a deeply satisfying laughter and suggests the true comedy others merely echo.

Sudden eruptions of laughter are like tiny sparks bursting forth from a mighty bonfire called joy—a blazing flame that finds its source in a joyous God.

Shortly before his death in 1321, a man named Dante Alighieri completed an epic poem destined to become the most influential work of its type ever penned. Written over a nearly twenty-five year period, his three volumes eventually were compiled into a single work known as *The Divine Comedy*. This medieval masterpiece of Catholic imagination chronicles Dante's journey through the hell of Inferno, the purification of Purgatory, and the ultimate joy of Paradise.

Those who have read Dante might wonder why anyone would ever call it a comedy. One looks in vain for jokes. And while I suppose some of the humor might get lost in translation from the original Latin, few scenes draw even a smile, let alone laughter. Dante purposefully chose the word "comedy" in contrast to the word "tragedy". His story, like his theology, has a happy ending after a dreadful beginning. The pain of bad eventually gets overtaken by the surprise of good. The laughter comes not in response to slapstick humor, but in response to unspeakable joy—the misery of human failure undone by the cheer of divine redemption. In short, the true bonfire of delight, made even more delightful by the temporary sorrows we endure.

Without God, the story of life is, by definition, tragedy. Without a divine comedian, we have no one to write in the surprise of joy. Oh sure, we can manufacture the cynical laugh of satire, or the sick joke of cruelty, as children mercilessly tease the outcast. But such attempts at laughter feel empty at best, warped at worst. They fail to scratch our itch for happiness, and dim rather than reflect the divine spark within every human being. The truly great comic remains both positive and wholesome. Laugh with Bill Cosby and you feel refreshed. Laugh with Eddie Murphy and you feel ashamed.

Dante, like the Stooges and Grandpa Grey, remind me that we are not meant to take our current experience too seriously. Yes, we may suffer the inferno today, but the surprise of Paradise is yet to come. A comedian writes the story of reality. He can use serious scenes as a set-up for unexpected laughter. The darker our days, the more we yearn to laugh—not in order to escape reality, but to connect with it.

God is not a cruel prankster enjoying our pain, but a truly gifted comedian, One who delights in our happiness. He does not laugh at us. He laughs with us.

GOING DEEPER

Use the following to prompt further reflection, or to facilitate a group discussion.

The psalms frequently call us to joy and celebration in response to the invasion of salvation. (See Psalm 21:1, 27:6, 30:5, 32:11, 51:12, and 126:5.)

- Why do you think David and other Old Testament characters referred to the joy of salvation long before the coming of the Messiah?

- How does anticipation and expectation change our ability to "laugh" in the midst of real-world difficulties?

In Luke 2:10 we learn that an angel declared "good tidings of great joy which will be to all people" (NKJV) and in Luke 6:21 Jesus said "Blessed are you who weep now, for you shall laugh."

- Think of a time when the "surprise" of joy overtook a time of great fear, worry, sorrow, or pain in your life (i.e. pain of childbirth forgotten upon seeing face of newborn baby; worry over health concern relieved by positive test results). Why is the laugher of relief so satisfying after the nervous laughter of fear or uncertainty?

In Luke 15:10 Jesus applies the parable of the lost coin to our situation by saying, "There is joy in the presence of the angels of God over one sinner who repents."

- What does this story suggest about the centrality of salvation to healthy, joy-filled laughter?

4

Blinding Light
What Shadows Suggest

It is the day of my nephew's graduation ceremony with about twenty-five or thirty friends and relatives attending the drop-in reception. I am walking a cranky Nicole to the park and back, a much-needed break for the baby and for me, and an opportunity to digest what I've experienced mingling with the crowd.

It is a happy event, an occasion to celebrate a high-school graduate's accomplishment and future. (I'll call him Mark to conceal identities.) Mark will head off to Columbia University in the fall, the first in his family to go Ivy League. All feel glad for him: lots of congratulating and well-wishing. Coordinated paper plates and punch cups and the obligatory bundle of helium-filled balloons tied to the back of one chair provide the perfect setting for uninteresting small talk and forced smiles. But below the surface of pleasant chatter and Mark's bright future, I sense dark shadows in the lives of one person after another.

Mark's mother, who I'll call Jill, has a hard time focusing on the guests. Her older boy is demanding attention, as usual. Hard to blame him, since visiting his mother is a special treat these days. The young man has lived in a group home for the handicapped since he became an adult, allowing Jill to have a life beyond the constant care-giving that defined his childhood years. I remember watching her in those days. She worked with her son so that he could learn to communicate despite near total blindness and significant hearing loss. Jill seemed the model of ruthless compassion, determined to help her son become the best his limitations would allow. In much the same way, she insisted that the younger Mark become all that his exceptional gifts would enable. Today, the contrast between them is stark. If Mark shines the light of great potential, his older brother casts the shadow of severe limitation.

A woman I'll call Charity is one of Mark's long-time neighbors. Very nice of her to drop by: especially in light of her recent struggles. She wears a lovely wig that covers what would otherwise announce her chemotherapy and radiation treatments. If you didn't know about her cancer, you wouldn't be able to tell. "I've just completed my second round," she says.

It's difficult to go through something so traumatic and have people unaware.

"It seems to have been successful. I'm in remission." A hopeful sign, but the word *seems* keeps a chill in the air.

"That's wonderful news," comes the expected reply. "You look great!" What to say when you don't know what to say. "Well, good to see you."

Conversation over: not because Charity doesn't want to talk about it, but because others don't know how.

Another neighbor I'll call Brad also attends. Slightly older than Mark, his own graduation propelled him into the real world several years earlier. But the world eagerly opening its arms to Mark has been less welcoming to Brad, due to his severely deformed face. Several surgeries have helped, like positioning hearing aids where there should be ears. But they don't cover as well as Charity's wig. Inadequate facial bone structure creates the appearance of one who has been either beaten, burned, or both. His face frightens my children. In truth, it probably frightens most adults.

Shaun, ten years old, overreacts in embarrassing shock. "I hope I didn't hurt his feelings…" he says in regret.

I wonder whether countless others, caught by surprise over the years, share that regret. I suppose one in Brad's situation gets used to it. But then, maybe they don't.

Things take a positive turn with Roger and Teresa: newlyweds married less than six months. I've known Teresa for years, my wife's forever single cousin. Suddenly, in her forties, she found Mr. Right. Roger seems very nice. A teacher and church worker, his quiet warmth seems impossible to dislike, unless you are his ex-wife. She left him for another man, abandoning a long-term marriage and two children for the promise of a better life. She probably didn't find it. But she nonetheless left the shadow of three broken hearts in the wake of her chase. Maybe Teresa can spark light into what must be some very dark hearts.

Teresa's sister, Janelle, seems glad she could attend. She spends much of her time caring for her once-strong father who now suffers the ravages of Alzheimer's disease. My wife, Olivia, does the same for her own mother. Both enjoy this brief reprieve from the ongoing heartache and frustration understood only by those who bear the burden of an aging parent's care.

And then there is Mark's justifiably proud father. What could feel better than watching your youngest son move the graduation cap tassel and point his shining star toward one of the nation's most prestigious universities? To top it off, his older boy from a previous marriage seems to be doing well: working a good job, enjoying a lovely wife and kids. Despite Dad's smiling face, however, I wonder whether the joy of this day dims a bit at the memory of another day when one of his adult children died from an illness medical attention might have prevented. His son hadn't cared enough about life to bother with treatment, so death obliged. Its tragic knife must have driven deep into Dad's heart. Can any father completely celebrate the achievements of one son without grieving the loss of another?

As I carry Nicole back inside and re-enter the party, gifts have begun to be opened and cake enjoyed. Laughter fills the scene, all focused on the bright graduate with an even brighter future. And yet, knowing the dark shadows in the lives of those around him, I foresee the possibility of his own. I hope Mark's life will be filled with nothing but light. Unfortunately, like everyone else in the room, I know better.

Who made evil?

I recall the question posed by Shakespeare's great predecessor, poet and dramatist Christopher Marlowe. In his most famous play, *The Tragical History of Doctor Faustus*, Marlowe's central character, Dr. Faustus, confronts evil, personified in his antagonist, Mephistopheles. British playwright Dorothy Sayers powerfully captured his dilemma (and ours) in a contemporary retelling.

> *Faustus: Tell me, then, thou Evil, who made thee?*
>
> *Mephistopheles: He that made all things.*
>
> *Faustus: What? Did God make thee? Was all the evil in the world made by God? Beware what thou sayest; I know thee for a false and lying spirit.*[14]

Faustus, like most of us, jumps quickly to God's defense. He cannot accept the notion that God might not be good. Nor can we. Even as we shake an accusing fist at heaven over some disappointment, we secretly hope He isn't to blame.

But wishful thinking comes up short, and the question still haunts us. Philosophers and theologians have long debated the nature of evil. Is it real or an illusion? Is it an actual thing, or merely the absence of something else? Did God make it, or did it come into being of its own accord? And if so, does that make God something less than omnipotent? After all, if he is all good and all-powerful, shouldn't He have prevented evil's birth?

These questions get cast in an entirely new light, however, when Faustus poses the direct query we all yearn to ask.

> *Faustus: Answer again, and this time all the truth, art thou God's henchman or His master? Speak! Who made thee?*

Mephistopheles: God, as the light makes the shadow.

Faustus: Is God, then, evil?

*Mephistopheles: God is only light, and in the heart of
the light, no shadow standeth, nor can I dwell within the
light of Heaven where God is all.*[15]

Mephistopheles then explains that true light cannot create
darkness. But anything that turns its back on light will see its
own dark shadow.

I can see only two real options.

Option one: a good God exists who allows His creation to
turn its back on His light. Those who embrace this option see
the shadow, driving them to seek the light.

Option two: evil rules the universe. Those who embrace
this option see only darkness, and it drives them mad.

Blame the devil's rebellion, Adam's fall, or whatever source
you wish. One thing is certain: you and I see the shadow,
something that can exist only in the presence of light.

I am the light

Hers was a life so full of shadows she is universally known for her
shame rather than a name. We don't call her Rachel or Hannah
or Joy or Grace. Just "the woman caught in adultery." The last in
what must have been a long line of dehumanizing labels.

"Sweet thing."

"Little tramp."

"Dirty whore."

Had she been victimized as a child, and abandoned to a life of prostitution? Or had she naïvely given herself to a man promising to leave his wife? We don't know. All we know is what the Scriptures tell us.

She was having sex with a man when religious leaders stormed into the room. She must have looked for something with which to cover herself. Perhaps the men had already retrieved her trail of discarded clothes, quickly gathering evidence while enjoying the view.

She blushed in shame.

Or did she curse in defiance?

"Hypocrites!" she may have shouted, while pointing toward the room filled with prior clients. "How dare you act as if you're better than me!"

But that is precisely what they did. The Scriptures describe the scene.

> *Then the scribes and Pharisees brought a woman caught*
> *in adultery, making her stand in the center. "Teacher,"*
> *they said to Him, "this woman was caught in the act of*
> *committing adultery.["]*[16]

They dragged her into the middle of a crowd that had gathered to hear Jesus teach. The same crowd that had once listened to them: even admired them. But that was before this wandering preacher from Nazareth called them a "brood of vipers" and questioned their wisdom. Not to mention their integrity.

Looking up, the woman must have felt an intense fear rise in her throat. Her pitiful life was about to end with the crushing blow of countless stones, some of which would be thrown by men who had used her like a toy. Who were using her again.

> *"Teacher," they said to Him, "this woman was caught in the act of committing adultery. In the law Moses commanded us to stone such women. So what do You say?" They asked this to trap Him, in order that they might have evidence to accuse Him.*[17]

You know the story. Jesus doodled in the sand with His finger. They pressed Him for an answer. He stood up and turned the tables on them.

> *"The one without sin among you should be the first to throw a stone at her."*[18]

Moments later, the woman's accusers backed off. Speechless, one by one, they had all slinked away. But the crowd remained. So did the teacher.

> *"Woman, where are they? Has no one condemned you?"*

> *"No one, Lord," she answered.*

> *"Neither do I condemn you," said Jesus. "Go, and from now on do not sin anymore."*[19]

It is in this context that Jesus turned to the people and spoke some of His most inspiring and offensive words.

> *"I am the light of the world. Anyone who follows Me will never walk in darkness but will have the light of life."*[20]

Inspiring because Jesus lets us in on a secret about Himself. A secret the apostle John described in the opening scene of his Gospel.

> *The true light, who gives light to everyone, was coming into the world. He was in the world, and the world was created through Him, yet the world did not recognize Him.*[21]

Offensive for reasons Jesus Himself had explained in an earlier conversation with a member of the religious establishment.

> *"This, then, is the judgment: The light has come into the world, and people loved darkness rather than the light because their deeds were evil."*[22]

Those gathered around Jesus and the one caught in adultery must have reacted in horror to the same declaration that gave the woman hope. "Is he saying what I think he's saying?"

He was. Jesus claimed to be the light of the world. The person whose first recorded words are "Let there be light." The person who invented Adam's cornea and later used dirt and spittle to give sight to the blind. And the person who promised, "anyone who lives by the truth comes to the light."[23]

The woman caught in adultery had a life temporarily dimmed by the silhouette of sin. But she was offered a dignifying hope. "Neither do I condemn you. Go, and from now on do not sin anymore."

The religious leaders' hearts were permanently darkened by the rejection of truth.

Walking in the light is a choice.

So is living in the shadows.

GOING DEEPER

Use the following to prompt further reflection, or to facilitate a group discussion.

The story of man's fall as told in Genesis 3 describes abusing the good gift of our freedom to choose.

- Read Genesis 2:25 and Genesis 3:7. Why do you think the Scriptures identify shame as the first "shadow" associated with our rebellion against light?

- How would the human experience be different if we saw one another as works of art to cherish rather than objects to use?

Read Genesis 1:3, John 1:3–5, and John 12:46.

- Why is it significant that God's first act of creation was light?

- How does understanding the words of John 1:3–5 and John 12:46 help us keep the dark shadows of a fallen world in proper perspective?

1 John 1:5–7 connects the dots between God's light and our shadows. 1 Peter 2:9 describes our call to leave darkness to enter "His marvelous light" (NKJV).

- Since there is no darkness in God, how can there be darkness in our world, according to these passages?

- What are the implications of knowing God has called you from darkness to light?

5

First Cause
Where Pain Points

As I entered the lecture hall lobby, an uptight man standing behind a folding table scattered with books and leaflets greeted me. At first, I mistook him for one of those religious fanatics who wave signs with misspelled words while barking at people. He certainly looked the part: a strange blend of quirky college professor and scruffy, homeless drunk. As it turned out, however, this man was no zealous believer. He was a zealous unbeliever, something that became apparent when I glanced at his selection of material.

He had about six books from Prometheus Press, a well-known atheist publishing house, and several small tracts like the kind a street evangelist might distribute or a thickheaded Christian might give the waitress instead of a tip. But these tracts weren't created by believers to convert nonbelievers. They had been written from a nonbeliever to Christians. I thumbed through one of the leaflets, taking advantage of the idle moments before the event began.

The writer clearly viewed my faith as mere wishful thinking, like a child who invents a pretend playmate to avoid loneliness. I read on as the attacks moved from my intellect to whether my God is worth the effort. My atheist was starting to sound like one of those barking sign-wavers. Still, he got me thinking: but only for a moment. My reading was interrupted when the moderator approached the microphone to begin the main event: a debate jointly hosted by the "Internet Infidels" and "Free Thinkers" at Colorado College. The topic: *Does God Exist?*

Each participant had a Ph.D. behind his name. Both taught philosophy at the university level. Each had examined the evidence, and come to dramatically different conclusions. One described himself as a theist, the other an atheist. Actually, not a true atheist. By his own admission, it is impossible to prove a universal negative, such as the statement, "There is no God." So, rather than try to defend an indefensible position, he described himself as agnostic, one who believes we cannot know whether God exists.

For the next ninety minutes, each gentleman presented his case. The theist described how, while we may not be able to prove God's existence, the evidence for it seems much stronger than the evidence against it, making it the more reasonable position. The agnostic, on the other hand, presented the reasons for his lack of belief, such as the problem of evil. After respectfully listening to one another, each challenged the other's points.

I found watching the audience of about 200 more interesting than the debate itself. From their nonverbal reactions to the presentation, I discerned three distinct groups. First, I noticed those predisposed to reject God's existence, such as the book table man I met in the lobby. I also observed those predisposed to believe in God, many of whom seemed to be members of the campus Christian club. Both groups responded positively to the debater with whom they agreed while disregarding or disparaging the other. But a third smaller group seemed sincerely interested in both views. This handful of folks took notes, paused to reflect upon the statements made for and against, and mentally sorted through points and counterpoints—seemingly eager to grapple with life's most profound question.

After a brief break, the moderator moved into the final segment of the event, when the audience could ask questions.

Comments from the crowd confirmed my earlier impressions. The sincerely curious asked the best questions. The others displayed more demagoguery than inquiry, trying to convert the ignorant heathen or blaming believers for the Inquisition. Neither seemed very impressive, or effective.

Perhaps the most dramatic moment of the evening came when a woman approached the microphone, barely able to contain her anger. Thus far questions had been posed in a respectful tone despite strong disagreement. Not this time. Probably in her early fifties, she looked much older, as if life had dealt her some very hard blows. She pointed an accusing finger and unloaded a lifetime of resentment upon God's defender.

"I want to know where this God of yours is when little children are abused, or when people are buried under the rubble of buildings destroyed by wartime bombs!" Her face grew increasingly red as her volume increased. "I can't believe in a God that passively sits back and watches innocent people suffer." While her examples came from other sources, her passion betrayed a painful personal story. She moved from general objections to a personal attack. "You seem pretty healthy and happy to me. I don't sense you know what it is to suffer, to endure great loss and disappointment! From where you sit, it is easy to believe in a good God."

What she didn't know is that the man she accused of glibly presenting a good God without personal knowledge of pain was, in fact, suffering the greatest heartache of his life. His beloved wife, the mother of their two small children, had been enduring the uncertain ravages of chemotherapy, and he faced the very real possibility of losing her.

After several minutes of bitter accusation, the moderator interrupted the woman in order to provide opportunity for a response. The crowd grew hushed, some hoping the theist had finally met his match, others eager to hear how he would answer a question that they could not.

"I would like to ask you," came the surprisingly calm reply, "to whom you express this anger you feel? The God I know would welcome an opportunity to comfort you, as He does to many who suffer as you've described."

Nice, but not really an answer.

He continued. "You are right to feel a sense of outrage at the evil in our world. But your outrage poses a very important question. Upon what basis do you call one thing wrong and another right? Unless there is such a thing as good, we would not be able to recognize bad. So, your anger at evil points to the existence of the good, a perfect good that has its source in a perfect God."

Remarkable! He used the problem of evil as evidence for rather than against the reality of God. Yes, evil exists in our world. But without God, the ultimate standard of good, we have no basis upon which to condemn it. In short, every "ought *not* be" points to the greater reality of an "ought *to* be."

The anger of that woman and the book table tract man suddenly made perfect sense. They both had recognized the heart's suspicion that something is wrong. Expressing outrage at the cruelty of a broken world is perfectly appropriate. The problem is not in the anger, but in what we do with it. These people did not become atheists because they couldn't find evidence of a God. They became atheists because they wanted revenge.

Yale Ph.D. and University of Texas philosophy teacher J. Budziszewski can relate. He too was an angry atheist. He too pointed an accusing finger at those he considered mere wishful thinkers. In his words:

> *Because I believed things that filled me with dread, I thought I was smarter and braver than the people who didn't believe them. I thought I saw an emptiness at the heart of the universe that was hidden from their foolish eyes. Of course I was the fool.*[24]

Today, he describes his folly as something motivated by anger. "Disbelieving in God was a good way to get back at Him for the various things which predictably went wrong in my life after I had lost hold of Him."[25]

Like many others, Budziszewski knew life to be unfair. In suffering bad, he lashed out against the possibility of good. Of course, this created a problem. One can't cut the dead branch of evil from the tree of good while still seated on its limb. When we reject the good that God is, all that remains is the evil that He isn't.

"I knew that if there existed a horrible, there had to exist a wonderful of which the horrible was the absence. So my walls of self-deception collapsed all at once."[26]

Nineteenth-century poet and painter Rossetti once said that the worst moment for the atheist occurs when he feels really thankful and has nobody to thank. I believe the reverse is also true. When we grow angry at the pain of life, we need someone to whom we can express outrage and seek comfort.

I encountered a profound insight at that debate. I learned that our anger at bad suggests our desire for good, a good that can come only from God. When we reject His existence, we are like a hurt child screaming, "Get away from me!" at the parent eager to console. In truth, we fume at the pain and we wish God would protect us from its reach, and alleviate its touch. But that's something He can only do for those who believe He exists and that He is good enough to care.

Letters from the Earth

Once the most famous American writer in the world, Samuel Clemens (better known as Mark Twain) mastered ironic humor with a cynical twist. Propelled to notoriety by stories featuring Tom Sawyer and a mischievous misfit named Huck Finn, Twain offered a distinctive voice among the giants of his day including Charles Dickens, Leo Tolstoy, Victor Hugo, and Fyodor Dostoevsky. While these and other literary masters confronted social ills, Mark Twain poked fun at social quirks, including the simplistic faith of his fellow Americans.

Twain's subtle jabs at Christianity surface throughout many of his books, mostly as naïve conversations between or reflections of his most lovable characters. One of my favorites is when Huckleberry Finn tries to sort out the point of praying.

> *Then Miss Watson she took me in the closet and prayed, but nothing come of it. She told me to pray every day, and whatever I asked for I would get it. I tried it. Once I got a fish-line, but no hooks. It warn't any good to me without hooks. I tried for the hooks three or four times, but somehow I couldn't make it work. By and by, one day, I asked Miss Watson to try for me, but she said I was a fool. She never told me why, and I couldn't make it out no way.*
>
> *I sat down, one time, back in the woods, and had a long think about it. I says to myself, if a body can get anything they pray for, why don't Deacon Winn get back the money he lost on pork? Why can't the widow get back her silver snuffbox that was stole? Why can't Miss Watson fat up? No, says I to myself, there ain't nothing in it.*[27]

Twain's books are filled with similarly playful satire. Below the surface, however, lurked a much darker contempt, revealing itself more plainly in later writings.

For several decades after his death, Mark Twain's daughter, Clara Clemens, resisted the release of her father's short book titled *Letters from the Earth*. Once published, the reason for her apprehension became clear. The book sheds light on a side of her father better left in the shadows of obscurity. It revealed a bitter, deeply cynical man eager to spew venom at the God of Christianity.

The book presents a series of letters written by Lucifer to his angelic colleagues, Michael and Gabriel. Lucifer is not a fallen rebel, but an angel in good standing who visits the earth many generations after the Creator wound our world's clock and left it to its own devices. Lucifer sends back reports of how the odd inhabitants of this little planet have evolved, including the imaginative religion they have concocted. In his first letter, for example, Lucifer shares what he has discovered…

> *Moreover—if I may put another strain upon you—he thinks he is the Creator's pet. He believes the Creator is proud of him; he even believes the Creator loves him; has a passion for him; sits up nights to admire him; yes, and watch over him and keep him out of trouble. He prays to Him, and thinks He listens. Isn't it a quaint idea?… I must put one more strain upon you: he thinks he is going to heaven!… He has salaried teachers who tell him that. They also tell him there is a hell, of everlasting*

*fire, and that he will go to it if he doesn't keep the
Commandments.*[28]

Lucifer goes on to describe the heaven we've imagined, where we will spend forever doing what we don't like, such as singing and playing harps, and where what we most like, sexual intercourse, doesn't exist.

Twain wrote *Letters from the Earth* after the death of a child he considered the apple of his eye. She became ill during a world speaking tour forced upon him by financial ruin. He hated speaking tours, but debts mounted and he needed the cash. Twain received word of his daughter's illness while he was thousands of miles from America. He wanted desperately to comfort and nurture his precious girl, but could not reach home in time. She died, and they lowered her cold body into the ground while a grieving Twain grudgingly peddled his celebrated wit to the highest paying audiences.

Even though Twain was surrounded by devout Christian believers, or maybe because of it, he pulled no punches when it came to their object of faith, Jesus Christ. He didn't buy the image of a God kinder and gentler than the harsh, Old Testament lawgiver. If anything, Jesus made things worse. As Twain's Lucifer explains…

> *Now here is a curious thing. It is believed by everybody
> that while he was in heaven he was stern, hard, resentful,
> jealous, and cruel; but that when he came down to earth
> and assumed the name Jesus Christ, he became the*

opposite of what he was before: that is to say, he became sweet, and gentle, merciful, forgiving, and all harshness disappeared from his nature and a deep and yearning love for his poor human children took its place. Whereas it was as Jesus Christ that he devised hell and proclaimed it! … Which is to say, that as the meek and gentle Savior he was a thousand billion times crueler than ever he was in the Old Testament—oh, comparably more atrocious than ever he was when he was at his very worst in those old days![29]

Lucifer concludes Twain's heckling by declaring the God of Christianity a conscienceless moral bankrupt.[30]

Some of the material is light and playful. But it quickly turns dark, such as his description of the commandments God has supposedly given…

He says, naively, outspokenly, and without suggestion of embarrassment: "I the Lord thy God am a jealous God."

You see, it is only another way of saying, "I the Lord thy God am a small God; a small God, and fretful about many things."

He was giving a warning: he could not bear the thought of any other God getting some of the Sunday compliments of this comical little human race—he wanted all of them for himself.[31]

And one that seems directly linked to Twain's own loss…

*According to the belief of these people, it was God himself
who said: "Thou shalt not kill." Then it is plain that he
cannot keep his own commandments.*[32]

When faced with life's pain, Sam Clemens saw only darkness. His hope in the possibility of a good God died when his precious daughter took her last breath. He, like many, hit the wall of despair harder than expected. It happens all the time, prompting some of the most common and difficult questions in human experience.

"Why do bad things happen to good people?"

"How can a good God allow suffering?"

"Why is there evil in our world?"

Mark Twain, like the rest of us, encountered life's "ought not" that points to the "ought" at the heart of reality. His loss screamed that he was living in a broken world. That something is *wrong*, which is only possible if something *right* exists. That something is God, the first cause of all things, including a universal expectation that good, not evil, should be in charge.

GOING DEEPER

Use the following to prompt further reflection, or to facilitate a group discussion.

Read John 11:1–44 to see the context of the shortest verse in the Bible that says "Jesus wept."

- Why do you think Jesus cried upon seeing His friends grieve?

- What does Jesus' tears in response to life's pain tell us about God's reaction to human suffering?

- What can we learn from Jesus' explanation of his delay in verses 40–42? Which is the greater tragedy? Suffering or deception? Death or unbelief?

In John 9:1–41 we read the story of Jesus healing a man who had been born blind.

- In verses 2–3 we read that Jesus corrected the disciples' assumption that the man's blindness is the direct consequence of personal sin. What does Jesus' alternative explanation tell us about how God redeems pain and suffering?

- In verses 39–41, after the religious leaders try to discredit the miracle, Jesus explains that in God's economy of things a blind man who believes sees better than a seeing man who doesn't. What does this suggest about the importance of God's rescuing us from suffering versus trusting God in suffering?

Read the story of Joseph comforting his fearful brothers after they mistreated him in Genesis 50:15–22.

- Most of us ask God why He doesn't prevent our suffering. How does Joseph's perspective on his own mistreatment inform your response to the unfair and difficult circumstances in your own life?

6

Jealous Husband
Why God Seems Angry

"Should I forgive her?"

I couldn't respond right away. My distraught friend was on the other end of the line. He had just told me that his wife had confessed to having had a prolonged affair with a younger man. "She's sick with guilt," he explained. My buddy was paralyzed with shock and confusion.

How to answer? I imagined myself in his shoes. It made me nauseous. Furious.

I knew what I should say as a pastor. I should tell him to forgive, to find a counselor who could help them restore the relationship. But as his friend I wanted to say, "No way! Throw her out. Make her pay."

I forced the pastoral response through clenched teeth.

"You have a right to divorce her because she committed adultery," I began. "But God may call you to take her back and, in the process, model His own marriage to an unfaithful woman. Like the prophet Hosea."

To his credit, my friend chose the path of forgiveness and restoration. But my soul ached for one who now understood something of what God has endured.

Earlier I described how becoming a parent changed and informed my perception of God. He is a father who, like every good parent, can't help loving his children. Just as fatherhood gave me a fresh perspective on God's character and heart, falling in love with and marrying my wife, Olivia, gave me a small taste of the kind of passion and intense love my own merely reflects.

To understand why God sometimes seems angry, we must remind ourselves of key scenes in a love story in which we play a central role.

Scene One: God creates His beloved

So God created man in His own image, in the image of God He created him; male and female He created them. (Genesis 1:27 NKJV)

The Lord God formed the man from the dust of the ground and breathed into his nostrils the breath of life, and the man became a living being. (Genesis 2:7)

Many of us have read and reread the biblical account of man's creation to the point that it has become quite familiar. Perhaps too familiar. We have such limited comprehension of what was taking place at the moment mankind took that first breath.

This was perhaps the most thrilling moment in all eternity for God. After all, He was not just making another creature. He was meeting His future bride.

The closest we can come to understanding this scene in the drama is to recall "boy meets girl" scenes from other famous stories.

The moment Romeo's heart skipped a beat upon meeting the lovely Juliet.

The day Captain von Trapp found himself inexplicably attracted to Maria in *The Sound of Music*, unable to take his eyes off her inner and outer beauty.

When "Sleepless in Seattle" Tom Hanks spots Meg Ryan in the airport and later atop the Empire State Building – certain she is the woman who will fill the void in his heart.

That first nervous date when I fell madly in love with the woman I have been married to for over thirty years.

These and other scenes reflect a moment in God's story when everything changed.

I wonder if His heart skipped a beat.

I bet He couldn't take His eyes off her beauty.

Who knows what would have gone through the mind of God at the moment His beloved entered His life? One thing is certain. Nothing would ever be the same again.

Have you ever had a crush on someone? There is nothing quite so wonderful and awful. The thrill of their presence, even their voice. You notice everything: how she dresses, how he walks. The upward or downward curve of an eyebrow can make or ruin your week. Being anxious over the uncertainty, hoping they will notice you, perhaps even like you. And maybe someday love you. Remember getting tongue-tied in the middle of an ordinary conversation about some insignificant topic? You so wanted to make a good impression that you made a fool of yourself. At least that's the way it felt.

I kind of think this is a bit of what it was like for God during those first days with Adam and Eve. After all, mankind was given a free will: able to accept or reject God's affection. He loved them more than a new mother loves her infant, more than a newlywed loves his bride. He knew everything there was to know about them – more than they knew themselves. But He could not, would not, come on too strong. He wanted an intimacy that only occurs when both parties choose it. They could not be forced, compelled, or manipulated into such a love. They had to be drawn.

Can you imagine what it must have been like for Adam and Eve? Everything was new to them. Like a newborn babe trying to understand his surroundings, but with full capacity for understanding all they encountered. It had to be overwhelming, and exhilarating! Basking in the tender care of their Creator, walking hand-in-hand with Him "in the cool of the day" (Genesis 3:8 NKJV) and enjoying the sights, sounds, smells, and tastes of a virgin world. God and his beloved were like a couple on their first date, discovering just how wonderful the other can be.

Scene 2: A villain's plot

No matter how powerful, brave, or noble the hero, he becomes vulnerable to defeat when he loves another. A window of opportunity opens for an unscrupulous enemy to gain an unfair advantage in the battle.

Capture his child and threaten harm if demands aren't met.

Rape his bride, turning him into a madman driven by rage rather than a warrior disciplined by calculated strategy.

Or better yet, steal away the affection of the one he seeks to save, undermining his resolve by turning the quest into a pointless pursuit.

Through one means or another, the object of a hero's love can become the key to a villain's victory. Lucifer, the mastermind behind all diabolical brilliance, invented the strategy. As soon as God gave His heart to another, Satan began seeking his opportunity to use it for his advantage.

Lucifer was no fool. It was clear that he lacked the strength to challenge God's vastly superior might. So he plotted to change the nature of the conflict. With the creation of God's beloved, Lucifer's opportunity had come. He would use something good as a tool for ill. Evil is unable to create anything original. It is only able to twist and pervert that which God has created. As darkness is the absence of light and wrong the opposite of right, so choice could open the door to slavery by robbing it of true freedom. Passionate love could be twisted into empty indulgence by changing its object from another to the self. God could be changed from lover to oppressor by making the tree a sign of deprivation rather than a symbol of affection.

What is true freedom? To many, inspired by Lucifer's rebellion, it is rejecting all form of authority. Being master of one's own destiny, god of one's own life. But there is a catch. With rejection of God-ordained authority comes slavery to one's own passions and limitations. No longer able to choose good, such "freedom" is left with nothing but the marred scraps of evil.

True freedom is the ability to choose from the countless good gifts of God, that which He created for us to experience without guilt or consequence. Unspoiled by rebellion against beauty and goodness, free to enjoy pleasures made for deep fulfillment rather than empty enslavement. Lucifer's plot was a stroke of diabolical brilliance. By changing the good of freedom into the evil of slavery, he could steal away the heart of one in order to break the heart of another.

Scene 3: Apple conspiracy

Next comes a defining scene behind our understanding of God the jealous husband. It is the moment when the plots of the seen and the unseen worlds collide. The once-trusted servant turned rebel enters time and space to approach God's innocent beloved. Wrapped in the form of the most mysterious creature in the garden, and drawing upon the faint echo of beauty residing within his otherwise corrupt existence, he seduces her with sweet-sounding deceptions.

A fulfilled, cherished bride who trusts her husband cannot be seduced away. But if she believes that trust has been violated, she may seek comfort in the arms of another. Lucifer had to cause Adam and Eve to question the affection and trustworthiness of their God. Twisting truth into a question, he very intentionally plants the idea that God's true desire was to withhold more from them than they realized.

Now the serpent was more crafty than any of the wild
animals the Lord God had made. He said to the woman,
"Did God really say, 'You must not eat from any tree in
the garden'?" (Genesis 3:1)

"*Any* tree in the garden?" God placed a restriction on only one tree. In fact, He clearly said they could eat of every other tree. Did Lucifer misspeak? Not at all. Read between the lines and discover his true intent. "One restriction is only the beginning. Why any restrictions at all? I'll tell you why! He is withholding more than you know. He is keeping you from your true destiny. Threatened by anyone who invades his domain of arrogance, He wants you to remain inferior in order to stroke His monstrous ego."

Responding to Eve's attempt to clarify the command, Lucifer paints God as One with less than noble intentions—One who may be less than trustworthy.

"You will not surely die," the serpent said to the woman.
"For God knows that when you eat of it your eyes will
be opened, and you will be like God, knowing good and
evil." (Genesis 3:4–5)

At this moment, two powerful forces converge: pleasure and deception. The first a good created by God. The second an evil conspired by Satan.

When the woman saw that the fruit of the tree was good
for food and pleasing to the eye, and also desirable for

gaining wisdom, she took some and ate it. She also gave
some to her husband, who was with her, and he ate it.
(Genesis 3:6)

It was good for food. It was pleasing to the eye. It would give wisdom. What could God have against such things? Perhaps he really was threatened, driven by arrogance, unworthy of their love.

Shaken by a lie. Driven by desire. The beloved enters the embrace of another.

God's enemy.

And her own.

Scene 4: Broken heart

Learning that your youngest child is dying of cancer.

Discovering your spouse in bed with another lover.

Helplessly watching as your teen sacrifices her innocence on the altar of rebellion.

Being falsely accused of a crime you didn't commit, by your best friend.

The agonizing pain of these tragic events combined into the greatest heartbreak ever known. God felt them all, and more, during the eternal tremor of mankind's fall.

Then the eyes of both of them were opened, and they
realized they were naked; so they sewed fig leaves
together and made coverings for themselves. Then the

> *man and his wife heard the sound of the Lord God as he*
> *was walking in the garden in the cool of the day, and they*
> *hid from the Lord God among the trees of the garden.*
> *But the Lord God called to the man, "Where are you?"*
> *(Genesis 3:7–9)*

"Where are you?" Three terrible words that said it all.

The days of walking hand-in-hand during the cool of the day, of intimate oneness, ended.

The pain of death and heartache of separation began.

I believe God wept from the knowledge of what His beloved would endure at the hand of His enemy. He grieved over the stench of impurity and mire of wickedness she would willingly embrace. Already sinking into the dark quicksand of sin's control, Adam admits several previously unknown feelings: fear, shame, and a desire to hide himself.

> *"I heard you in the garden, and I was afraid because I*
> *was naked; so I hid." And he said, "Who told you that*
> *you were naked? Have you eaten from the tree that I*
> *commanded you not to eat from?" (Genesis 3:10–11)*

Sinking further still, they blame others for their own willing choice.

> *And the man said, "The woman you put here with me—*
> *she gave me some fruit from the tree, and I ate it."…*
> *The woman said, "The serpent deceived me, and I ate."*
> *(Genesis 3:12–13)*

Knowledge beyond purity had come, and there was no turning back. The reality of life apart from God was now theirs, and it was a cold, dark, and barren place. Like the rebel who had lured them into his domain, Adam and Eve got what they craved. Whether or not they would like it was another matter.

We rarely consider what man's fall meant in the unseen realm. We focus instead upon the bad things introduced into the human experience such as sickness, pain, death, and sorrow. But what did it mean to the other two characters in our drama?

For Satan, this was his moment. Finally able to strike back for the humiliation he experienced after his failed uprising, Lucifer relished in his victory over the One he saw as an arrogant tyrant. Crazed with the madness of self-deception, Satan had been frustrated for some time with his inability to strike back. Too weak for a direct attack, yet too strong to accept his defeat, this was the perfect means of vengeance.

For God, it was like a knife through the heart. All at once, He lost that which had been so perfect. The wonderful honeymoon of intimacy between God and His beloved was destroyed as the bride was found in bed with another lover during the honeymoon. I wonder whether at that moment God regretted giving us a free will. Did He consider taking it back? Did He weep at the knowledge of the horrors we would experience in days to come? Did He wish He could protect us from our own folly by erasing the consequences of sin? Of course He did. But He couldn't. Not because He wasn't powerful enough, but because God is a lover, not a rapist. He refuses to force Himself onto anyone or push His way into our lives. Again, when we chose to reject the good that He is, we embraced all of the bad that He isn't. A reality that, more than anything else, must have been the cause of tremendous grief.

In the unseen realm, Satan laughed while God wept.

The fall

A tearful young woman takes a long shower, trying to wash away the shame she feels after her first illicit encounter. Be it the abuse of rape or voluntary infidelity, the loss of sexual innocence makes us feel dirty, violated, ashamed. But that same girl will have a very different reaction after a year of prostitution. A cold stare tells you her heart is resigned to the shame that now defines her existence. A seductive glance suggests an acquired taste for erotic pleasures. Dark shadows under her eyes and deep facial lines invade the soft, graceful beauty she once possessed. And loud, brazen laughter overtakes the gentle, pretty smile that was so charming just twelve months earlier.

This same pattern is the experience of the human race. When first introduced to the illicit pleasures of sin, there was a sick feeling in the pit of our stomach. Our innocence had been violated; raped by a villain, seduced by an adulterous lover. We were, at first, ashamed. But before long, we forgot what innocence was like, and began preferring our fallen state.

The sad reality of the fall is that we now crave that which should make us cry. The human race has been living in bondage to sin for so long that we cannot even remember the thrilling excitement and passion found in purity. Celebrating our addictions, we view them as keys of liberation rather than chains of enslavement.

In a fictitious series of letters between two demons, the elder Screwtape advises his nephew, Wormwood, on how to use God's invention of pleasure against us.

> *Never forget that when we are dealing with any pleasure in its healthy and normal and satisfying form, we are, in a sense, on the Enemy's ground. I know we have won many a soul through pleasure. All the same, it is His intention, not ours … Hence we always try to work away from the natural condition of any pleasure to that in which it is least natural, least redolent of its Maker, and least pleasurable. An ever increasing craving for an ever diminishing pleasure is the formula.*[33]

Our new "lover" has twisted the gift of desire into an affliction, driving us to things that kill rather than fulfill.

> *My bones have no soundness because of my sin. My guilt has overwhelmed me like a burden too heavy to bear. My wounds fester and are loathsome because of my sinful folly. (Psalm 38:3b–5)*

> *When you were slaves to sin, you were free from the control of righteousness. What benefit did you reap at that time from the things you are now ashamed of? Those things result in death! (Romans 6:20–21)*

But each one is tempted when, by his own evil desire,
he is dragged away and enticed. Then, after desire has
conceived, it gives birth to sin; and sin, when it is full-
grown, gives birth to death. (James 1:14–15)

This is the reality of every person born on earth. We all experience the enticement and enslavement of sin pulling us deeper into the abyss of self-gratification. "Ever increasing craving for an ever diminishing pleasure." But, unlike Lucifer, we are made in God's image. Our hearts were made to experience more. Like a caged bird, we long to soar. But we have forgotten who and what we were made to be.

That's why God, the jealous husband eager to redeem His beloved, confronts us with the truth of our condition. He wants to remind His people that idolatry is not merely exploring other religious options. It is betraying a sacred bond of intimate union.

No wonder God seems angry when reading certain Old Testament scriptures. Any other reaction would be unjust when you realize His bride has been lured into a life of prostitution.

Consider the words given to the prophets Jeremiah and Hosea when describing the actions of God's people.

"But you have played the harlot with many lovers;
yet return to Me," says the Lord. "Lift up your eyes to
the desolate heights and see: Where have you not lain
with men? By the road you have sat for them … you
have polluted the land with your harlotries and your
wickedness." (Jeremiah 3:1–2 NKJV)

"For you have played the harlot against your God. You have made love for hire on every threshing floor." (Hosea 9:1 NKJV)

Yes, God gets angry. But not the immature, petty jealousy of a teenage crush. His is the grieving, righteous response of the One who is too good to passively accept our enslavement to sin. In the words recorded by Jeremiah …

"Return, faithless people," declares the Lord, "for I am your husband. I will choose you … " (Jeremiah 3:14)

God is love. How we experience that love, however, is up to us: dreadful or beautiful, a gift to relish, or an obligation to despise.

GOING DEEPER

Use the following to prompt further reflection, or to facilitate a group discussion.

Read Jeremiah 2:19 – 3:25, where the prophet confronts the people of God with the painful truth of their waywardness.

- Reading the Old Testament prophets has been likened to listening to an angry husband shout at an unfaithful wife. What phrases give that impression here?

Read the entire book of Hosea.

- God calls Hosea to marry a harlot, and repeatedly buy her back from prostitution. How does Hosea's marriage symbolize God's marriage to us?

7

Uncensored Truth
Shouldn't God Watch His Language?

Believers don't need skeptics or hecklers to point out the unpleasant or embarrassing aspects of our faith. The Bible itself does a pretty good job of keeping us off balance. In fact, on more than one occasion I have found myself wishing God had held His tongue. Don't get me wrong; I believe and trust the Scriptures with all of my being. But certain portions still make me cringe.

Apparently, I'm not alone. A number of deeply committed Christians admit that certain Bible passages make them uneasy. I suppose that's why we rarely mention the harder sayings, gravitating to the more pleasant passages like the gentle shepherd of Psalms or "the greatest of these is love" from 1 Corinthians.

God would have a very different image had He let me describe Him to the human race. I would have presented Him as nicer, less prone to wrath, and more willing to overlook offense. I would have done a better job concealing aspects of His character that many consider disagreeable. I suppose that is why He wrote His own book and why He revealed Himself in person through the incarnation. God didn't want to be promoted and sold. He wanted to be known.

One of the reasons I believe in the God of the Bible is that He is much more than I want Him to be: Someone to fear, not just fancy. Someone willing to redeem, but entitled to condemn. Someone who said things I wish He hadn't. I can't imagine God as human invention, since in our desire to make Him better, we would have made Him less.

During conversations with many unbelievers, I have stumbled onto a surprising discovery. They have the impression that believers enthusiastically and unreservedly accept every difficult concept found in the Bible, welcoming truths any thinking or compassionate person would reject out of hand. I guess we do a pretty good job wearing our salesperson faces, since most seemed surprised to learn that many devout Christians, myself included, struggle with the harder sayings of Scripture. The fact that we believe them does not mean that we like them, or even fully understand them. Let's take a look at a few such gems.

"Sin is crouching at your door."

In the world's first incidence of sibling rivalry, a nice kid named Abel gets killed during his jealous brother's temper tantrum. A tragedy, for sure. But something even more disturbing surfaces when we learn what triggered Cain's wrath.

> *Now Abel kept flocks, and Cain worked the soil. In the course of time Cain brought some of the fruits of the soil as an offering to the Lord. (Genesis 4:2–3)*

So far, so good. Cain seeks to honor God with a portion of his bounty. Abel does likewise, offering the finest of his flock. Two good religious kids trying their best to worship the Lord as best they know how.

> *The Lord looked with favor on Abel and his offering,*
> *but on Cain and his offering he did not look with favor.*
> *So Cain was very angry, and his face was downcast.*
> *(Genesis 4:4–5)*

Can you blame him? Like a child holding up his best Crayola masterpiece, Cain must have anticipated Daddy's smiling approval. Instead, he received a frown.

> *Then the Lord said to Cain, "Why are you angry? Why*
> *is your face downcast? If you do what is right, will you*
> *not be accepted? But if you do not do what is right, sin is*
> *crouching at your door." (Genesis 4:6–7)*

We know the rest of the story. A dejected Cain lures his younger brother into an open field to take his life. If you can't color the best picture, eliminate the competition.

While we rightfully condemn Cain for murder, we also wonder why a God known as a loving Father rejected His child's well-intentioned offering. Wouldn't it be better if He accepted folks like Cain, even when they fail to meet His seemingly arbitrary criteria for proper worship? This passage seems to suggest that He is too persnickety for such approval, harshly condemning every sincerely expressed religion caught coloring outside the lines.

"Now kill all the boys."

Another biblical story that suggests our loving heavenly Father might have a dark side appears in the book of Numbers, when the Lord orders Moses to take vengeance on the Midianites for long-ago offenses against Israel. Characteristic of much Old Testament scripture, the story reflects an "eye for an eye" philosophy more than a "turn the other cheek" approach in its response to mistreatment.

> *They fought against Midian, as the Lord commanded Moses, and killed every man … The Israelites captured the Midianite women and children and took all the Midianite herds, flocks and goods as plunder. They burned all the towns where the Midianites had settled, as well as all their camps. They took all the plunder and spoils, including the people and animals … (Numbers 31:7–11)*

Harsh? It certainly seems like it. But war is hell, and we expect soldiers to overdo it when conquering enemy territory. At least they protected women and children in compliance with the guidelines of just war. Moses shouldn't be too upset with his soldiers.

In the next scene, however, Moses becomes quite angry. Not because they were too harsh, but because they were too gentle.

> *Moses was angry with the officers of the army … "Have you allowed all the women to live?" he asked them.*

"They were the ones who followed Balaam's advice and were the means of turning the Israelites away from the Lord in what happened at Peor, so that a plague struck the Lord's people. Now kill all the boys. And kill every woman who has slept with a man, but save for yourselves every girl who has never slept with a man." (Numbers 31:14–18)

The Israeli army is ordered to slaughter civilian women and children. So much for just war guidelines. One can only imagine the bloodbath Moses' order caused, pregnant girls and frightened little boys dying at the tip of a sword.

How do we reconcile this scene with the teachings of Jesus about loving our enemies and forgiving those who trespass against us? It is difficult. Which is why I list it among the portions of Scripture I wish could be ignored.

"Whoever does not believe stands condemned already..."

I understand why God would condemn Joseph Stalin or Adolf Hitler. Their willful defiance and crimes against humanity place them clearly in the "doomed" category. What is harder to accept, however, is universal condemnation as described by Jesus just after His trademark slogan "For God so loved the world" found in John 3:16.

Whoever believes in him is not condemned, but whoever does not believe stands condemned already because he

has not believed in the name of God's one and only Son.
(John 3:18)

Why didn't God program the system to work in our favor? Rather than default to eternal life, why did He set it to condemnation? To be forgiven one must believe. For damnation, however, no action required.

"But none are innocent," we might argue. "After all, Romans 3:23 tells us that all have sinned and fallen short of the glory of God."

Fine. So nobody's perfect. Does that mean all must be condemned? Why must the path to destruction be "wide" while the road to life so "narrow" that few can find it? (See Matthew 7:13–14.) On the surface of things, the whole system seems backward to us.

"No one comes to the Father except through me."

They may be the most disturbing two sentences Jesus uttered during His earthly ministry: nineteen words confronting us with a clear choice.

"I am the way and the truth and the life. No-one comes
to the Father except through me." (John 14:6)

There is no mistaking His meaning. Jesus did not leave us the option of viewing every sincere religious pursuit as equally valid. He did not offer Himself as one path among many to the same destination. Jesus described Himself as the only way to

God, end of story. Various world religions are not alternative routes. They are at best rabbit trails, at worst roads to hell paved with good intentions.

It is no exaggeration to place these two sentences among the most troubling tenets of Christian belief. Frankly, I sometimes wish we could hold a less exclusive view. It would be nice to view Jesus as one among many mystics, prophets, or avatars pointing us to God. I wish Cain's offering was as acceptable as Abel's. I would like to believe that Jews, Muslims, Mormons, Hindus, and Buddhists are all saying the same thing with different words. But Jesus did not leave that option, no matter how much I might wish He had.

"He must deny himself and take up his cross and follow me."

I recall a comment by a woman I interviewed named Sarah. She said that she liked the idea of God because it would bring comfort. Apparently, she hasn't heard one of Jesus' more unsettling declarations.

> *Then he called the crowd to him along with his disciples and said: "If anyone would come after me, he must deny himself and take up his cross and follow me. For whoever wants to save his life will lose it, but whoever loses his life for me and for the gospel will save it." (Mark 8:34–35)*

I wish Jesus hadn't said that. It disturbs Sarah's ideal of the warm, peaceful feelings associated with religious belief. You know the image: troubled folks escaping the harsh realities of life by believing in a loving God who leads us beside still waters and protects us through the valley of the shadow of death. Jesus' words instead suggest a God who shoves our face in the rapids of life while we struggle for air.

"If you want to live," comes the call of Christ, "give up your life!"

Not exactly the best marketing campaign if you hope to attract new converts. Not exactly the kind of religious comfort Sarah and others admire.

Christianity is anything but an escape to a pleasant stroll down easy street. It is an invitation to follow Jesus, One who bore a cross and gave His life for others. And no matter how unsettling it may seem, He expects the same from us.

"God chose the foolish..."

I like to think of myself as a reasonably intelligent person. I want to be perceived as perceptive and well read, a smarter than average guy who deserves the respect of the educated class. I listen to National Public Radio, watch the Discovery Channel on television, and rarely take tabloid headlines seriously. I see my Christian beliefs as reasonable, defensible, and built upon a solid foundation of archeological and historical evidence. I suppose that is why I become uneasy over certain New Testament descriptions of faith.

*Now faith is the substance of things hoped for, the
evidence of things not seen. (Hebrews 11:1 KJV)*

I don't like that definition. I want faith to be the rational response
to evidence that demands a verdict and proof that cannot
be refuted. But Scripture offers a very different description.
Unimpressed by brains and brawn, it celebrates characteristics
I would rather conceal than acknowledge.

*But God chose the foolish things of the world to shame
the wise; God chose the weak things of the world to
shame the strong. He chose the lowly things of this world
and the despised things—and the things that are not—
to nullify the things that are, so that no-one may boast
before him. (1 Corinthians 1:27–29)*

I don't much like that passage, either. It suggests that those
of us following Jesus are foolish, weak, and lowly, not wise,
strong, and exalted. I want to be listed among the best and the
brightest, to flaunt a high I.Q. and look down my nose at the
ignorant folly of unbelief. But God wants something different,
a posture that runs completely counter to my natural instinct.

*God opposes the proud but gives grace to the humble.
(James 4:6)*

Faith, no matter how much I want it to be otherwise, has
very little to do with what I know or how well I can defend

my beliefs. Christianity is not about articulately winning the argument over what is true. It is about humbly submitting the heart to what is real.

****

These are just a few examples where the editor of Scripture failed to temper God's language. As a result, you and I have been presented with who He is rather than what I might want Him to be. I am seminary-trained and own a large library of books that help me interpret each of the Bible's more troubling passages within a larger story and in light of explanatory context. But most believers throughout history have not had similar access or opportunity. They have had to rely on the raw, uncensored version.

We live in an age when image managers select the most flattering pictures to post, and put a positive spin on the most embarrassing actions of every celebrity. It seems to me those writing God's official book should have done something similar. But then I remember; God isn't a celebrity. He's an awful goodness.

GOING DEEPER

Read each of the passages referenced in this chapter and the following questions to prompt reflection, or to facilitate a group discussion.

- Genesis 1:31 – 2:3: How do we reconcile the claims of science that seem to contradict the teachings of scripture?

- Genesis 4:2–7: Does this passage leave room for the possibility that Cain had received prior instruction on the proper form of worship/sacrifice?

- Numbers 31:7–18: Some have suggested the Midianite society had become infested with diseases caused by sexual immorality that could have spread to the entire region if they were allowed to survive. How does this possibility change your impressions of Moses' order?

- John 3:16–21: Does the comment in verse 17 ("God did not send His Son into the world to condemn" NKJV) contradict verse 18 ("he who does not believe is condemned already" NKJV)? Why or why not?

- John 14:6–11: How does what Jesus says immediately after "No one comes to the Father except through Me" (NKJV) explain why any other option is impossible?

- Mark 8:34–35: Based upon Jesus' words in this passage, would you say Christianity is rooted in hard truth or feel-good religious sensibilities?

- 1 Corinthians 1:26–31: What is the reason God chooses to use the foolish and the weak?

8

Eternal Wrath
Does God Send People to Hell?

"How can you believe that?"

The conversation hadn't gone as I had hoped. What was supposed to be a loving invitation for my mother-in-law to accept Jesus as her personal savior got twisted into something else entirely. I'd thrown the lifeline to a drowning loved one, only to have her get tangled up in its line. The rope intended to rescue somehow got all wrapped around her neck. Was my toss or her struggle to blame?

"So anyone who doesn't believe the way you do is going to hell?" Her words squeezed through clenched teeth, revealing intensity forced under control. Clearly, the conversation had tapped a long emotional history with regard to Christianity. After all, the only "h" word I'd mentioned was heaven.

"How can you believe I am going to hell?" Tears of angry indignation flowed while I fumbled to redeem the conversation. But we had long passed the point of sharing "the good news of the gospel." No matter what I said, she remained fixed on one thought: Kurt is one of those insensitive Christians who believes she is condemned to eternal damnation.

Olive had good reason to react. We met when I began dating

her daughter, Olivia. I became a permanent fixture in her life when I married into the family, a family understandably leery of those who wear the label "Christian."

Only a few months before our little chat, my mother-in-law had experienced one of the most offensive confrontations imaginable: the kind that would give any unbeliever nightmares. She hesitantly accepted an invitation to a chapel service at the Baptist college her daughter attended, despite feeling uneasy about the high-pressure evangelism she had come to expect from fundamentalists. Olive had already rejected one form of Christianity, the Catholicism of her childhood. She had no interest in accepting another. And even if she had, it wouldn't be the Bible-thumping, *hellfire and brimstone* variety her daughter had somehow gotten caught up in. But Olivia was taking part in a special musical performance, and she really wanted her mother to attend. How can a parent say no? So Mom came and sat in the very back of the auditorium, eager to make a quick exit.

Neither mother nor daughter realized that there had been a set-up. The special chapel speaker that day was an old-style evangelist, the sort that took no prisoners. He believed all is fair in love, war and evangelism. Thanks to a tip from one of Olivia's concerned fellow students, the preacher knew an unbelieving mother would be in the audience. So he did the unthinkable. After proclaiming the hard truth of hell and the glorious hope of heaven, he pointed the verbal spotlight directly on Olivia's mother.

"I've been told that there is a mother here today who came to see her daughter perform."

The speaker's words sent a chill of cold terror darting through Olivia's body. *How does he know? Why in the world would he say such a thing from the platform? What would he say next?*

"Mom, you have a lovely child who desperately wants you to accept Jesus as your Lord and savior."

Olivia could do nothing. Her mother sat a dozen or more rows away; she had no way to explain that this was neither her idea nor doing. She could only hope it would end soon.

The preacher continued, "Don't you think it is time that you finally submit to the prompting of God's Spirit, and accept the gift of salvation He offers?"

After a few more appeals to Mom and any other "lost" in the crowd, the speaker wrapped up his portion of the service. Relieved the tense ordeal had finally ended, Olivia joined her fellow singers on stage to perform one final number. Then came the hard part, repairing the damage.

Unbelievably, things went from bad to worse. Much worse.

Just as Olivia reached her mother to begin post-service small talk before easing into an apology, the guest preacher approached to raise the bar with a direct, personal confrontation. Both Olivia and Mom got a deer in the headlights look as he began a process of rapid-fire evangelism at point-blank range. Emotions and defenses already high, the conversation quickly escalated. The preacher, visibly frustrated by Mom's stubborn resistance to the gospel, pulled out the heavy artillery.

"Madam, do you realize that if you die you will never see your daughter again, because she will be in heaven and you will be in hell?"

Both Mom and daughter burst into tears: Mom out of indignant rage, daughter out of perplexed shock. Years of gentle, loving attempts to show Jesus' love suddenly got blown out of the water by "kick butt" evangelism.

No wonder my mother-in-law resisted my effort to "share the good news." Even if her heart wanted to know, her mind couldn't help recalling Rambo the preacher. She suspects an evangelistic ambush designed to overwhelm her with one key message: "Madam, you are going to hell!"

She recalls a similar message growing up in a strict Catholic home. Olive tried to be a good girl, tried to follow the prescribed order of faith: mass, confession, rosary, and the rest. But something seemed askew. The faith that claimed to be the truth and the light had not, in her view, dispelled the lies and darkness within her own family. Being devout hadn't helped her father kick the bottle. Nor had it prevented her brother's death in what might have been suicide. Olive perceived her mother as one with an air of superiority rather than "meek, lowly, and humble of heart." It bothered Olive that her mother, like most in her social class, had little association with blacks, Jews, and Protestants.

Whether actual or merely perceived due to her own rebellious bent, Olivia's mom reacted against the faith of her parents. Not so much because she disagreed with or even understood its creeds, but because it was theirs. Yet for her, leaving the Catholic Church was the spiritual equivalent of jumping from a plane without a parachute. No matter how much fun you may have on the way down, you eventually reach bottom, where Dante's inferno awaits.

Despite leaving the church, its dogma never left her, including the nagging awareness that one cannot walk away with impunity. Even though she told herself she no longer believed in hell, it pursued her through the belief of others: father, mother, brother, and years later, daughter.

I've learned the hard way that it is important to listen before you speak when discussing faith. I wish I had known more of my mother-in-law's perceptions before we talked. I wish I had known about her hell hang-up before speaking of heaven. It would have been nice to know that no matter what I said, what she heard would first squeeze through a filter of bad experiences and conversations, none of which had painted an attractive picture of Christian belief.

The elephant in the room

There is an elephant in the room of Christian theology that cannot be ignored. It is big. It is ugly. And no matter how clear of its potentially crushing step one may stand, it makes us all uneasy. So we might as well face it directly. Jesus did—clearly and forcefully proclaiming its dreadful reality. Consider a few of His choice words.

> *You snakes! You brood of vipers! How will you escape being condemned to hell? (Matthew 23:33)*

> *The rich man also died and was buried. In hell, where he was in torment, he looked up and saw Abraham far*

away, with Lazarus by his side. So he called to him,
"Father Abraham, have pity on me and send Lazarus
to dip the tip of his finger in water and cool my tongue,
because I am in agony in this fire." (Luke 16:22–24)

The apostles also refer to it in their writings, such as Peter's frightening description of what awaits false teachers.

In their greed these teachers will exploit you with stories
they have made up. Their condemnation has long been
hanging over them, and their destruction has not been
sleeping. For if God did not spare angels when they
sinned, but sent them to hell, putting them into gloomy
dungeons to be held for judgment … if he condemned
the cities of Sodom and Gomorrah by burning them
to ashes, and made them an example of what is going
to happen to the ungodly … then the Lord knows
how to rescue godly men from trials and to hold the
unrighteous for the day of judgment, while continuing
their punishment … But these men blaspheme in
matters they do not understand. They are like brute
beasts, creatures of instinct, born only to be caught and
destroyed, and like beasts they too will perish. They will
be paid back with harm for the harm they have done. (2
Peter 2:3–13)

And don't forget John's prophetic summary of how our story ends.

> *And I saw the dead, great and small, standing before the*
> *throne, and books were opened … The dead were judged*
> *according to what they had done as recorded in the books*
> *… Then death and Hades were thrown into the lake of*
> *fire. The lake of fire is the second death. If anyone's name*
> *was not found written in the book of life, he was thrown*
> *into the lake of fire. (Revelation 20:12–15)*

Like it or not, Christianity includes the distasteful notion of eternal damnation. "Hellfire and brimstone" is more than a Southern Baptist preaching style. To those compelled to believe the teachings of Jesus and the apostles, it is the unthinkable destiny of millions.

As if the biblical descriptions were not bad enough, Dante Alighieri came along in the fourteenth century to craft an imaginative vision of the underworld that has literally scared the hell out of readers for generations. Its frightening portrait of a dark place specially designed to torment the heathen and punish the rebel creates a profoundly disturbing aura around the words "eternal damnation."

While touring the circular levels of hell, Dante encounters the anguished screams of the damned. His first journey includes a stroll through upper hell where unbelievers endure punishments specifically suited to their individual crimes. The lustful are blown about in a dark, stormy wind; the gluttonous endure filthy muck while battered with dirty hail, rain, and snow; and the slothful subsist beneath the mud, a bubbling surface the only indication of their endless suffocation below.

Moving further down the underworld tour, the narrator encounters the awful stench of lower hell, where the more serious suffering occurs. Heretics, sodomites, those who committed violence against others and against themselves through suicide, sorcerers, thieves, hypocrites, liars, traitors, and charlatans—all pay for their sins in this place of unrelenting horror and unquenchable fire. Dante's journey through hell's inferno ends when they reach the lowest region where Lucifer, frozen from the chest downward, devours the worst of human sinners…

> *In each of his three mouths he crunched a sinner,*
> *with teeth like those that rake the hemp and flax,*
> *keeping three sinners constantly in pain;*
>
> *the one in front—the biting he endured*
> *was nothing like the clawing that he took;*
> *sometimes his back was raked clean of its skin.*
>
> *"That soul up there who suffers most of all,"*
> *my guide explained, "is Judas Iscariot:*
> *the one with head inside and legs out kicking.*[34]

I feel more comfortable accepting the notion of hell when I think of Judas Iscariot or the perpetrators of the Holocaust. My soul cries out for such a place when reading of innocent girls brutally raped and dismembered by a deranged serial killer. As I said earlier, I don't want Hitler going to heaven. I want him to suffer for the unimaginable pain he caused.

On the other hand, when I think of loved ones who reject or ignore the gospel until their last breath, I want to interpret hell as mere allegory.

Mark struggles with the idea on both fronts. A committed Christian, he admits to a lifetime of wrestling with the concept of hell. A match he is losing, despite an otherwise traditional Protestant theology.

"The punishment doesn't fit the crime!" he almost shouts. His intensity tells me Mark has thought about this for some time. "I mean, even if a person spends seventy or eighty years living the most wicked existence imaginable, an eternity of torment seems extreme."

Mark is a compassionate person, a Christian counselor who ministers to people trapped in the addictive and destructive cycles of sin. He has a hard time condemning those he perceives unable to overcome the pull of evil. While responsible for their actions, he believes, they are still victims to the influence of human fallenness.

"For a person to suffer in flames forever and ever and ever," Mark continues, "how is God glorified in that?"

Many sidestep the harsh nature of biblical descriptions of hell by interpreting them as figurative or hyperbole. Mark would like to join them, but recognizes the problems of picking and choosing among Jesus' teachings, accepting those you like while explaining away the rest.

I recall the first time I grasped the concept of hell. I was a small child, probably too young for an R-rated concept like eternal damnation. Sitting in church beside my parents, my greatest fear had been getting caught teasing my brother, chewing the gum I was told to spit out before entering the service, or daydreaming rather than listening to the preacher. That fear quickly paled, however, by a much greater source of anxiety when the minister read what Jesus said about a threatening inferno.

> *If your hand causes you to sin, cut it off. It is better for you to enter life maimed than with two hands to go into hell, where the fire never goes out. And if your foot causes you to sin, cut it off. It is better for you to enter life crippled than to have two feet and be thrown into hell. And if your eye causes you to sin, pluck it out. It is better for you to enter the kingdom of God with one eye than to have two eyes and be thrown into hell, where "their worm does not die, and the fire is not quenched." (Mark 9:43–48)*

The prospect of worms that don't die and flames licking at scorchable flesh got my attention. But cutting off my hands and feet or poking out an eye seemed equally scary. Fortunately, the preacher gave me a much better alternative, suggesting I instead pray the sinner's prayer.

Decades later, my fears have shifted from my own eternal destiny to the destiny of others. It feels wonderful to be among millions who have accepted Jesus' gift of salvation, dodging worms and flames in the process. But billions have not, some of whom don't even know they have the option. What about *them*? How can I glibly accept the idea that they face such a dreadful demise?

For starters, I don't accept it glibly. On the contrary, eternal damnation is a sobering reality I hate to acknowledge and would love to deny. I believe it because Jesus taught it, not because I like it. As I said earlier, I wish I didn't believe some things in my theology. Hell is among the biggest.

The important question, however, is not whether I believe the hard sayings of the Bible, but why I do so despite disagreeable notions like eternal damnation.

I suppose I accept the hard sayings of Scripture for the same reason I pay $80 for thirty family photos of various sizes when I really only want the 8x10 and two wallets. You see, they come as a package. To get the two wallets I need to buy the rest, including more 5x7 photos than I have relatives.

Don't tell her I said so, but my wife has a few irritating habits. When we married, I happily accepted them as part of a wonderful package. Not all do. Some spouses accept only the pleasant parts of their mate and spend years rejecting, criticizing, or resenting the rest. Of course, doing so undermines and eventually destroys a relationship. In the process of spurning bad habits which will never disappear, we push away the good. As a result, the sweetness of wedded bliss gets displaced by the biting sting of endless conflict.

Truth comes as a package. I may want only the 8x10 of the Beatitudes, and the comfort of certain psalms. But to get them I must buy all of Christianity: redemption and damnation, grace along with wrath, "whosoever will" and its counterpart, "no other way."

We mustn't view Christianity like a pair of slippers: hoping it will be warm and cozy when we need a break from the harsh realities of life. C. S. Lewis once discouraged such thinking, acknowledging that parts of the Christian faith make one quite uncomfortable. In his words...

> *I wish it was possible to say something more agreeable. But I must say what I think true. Of course, I quite agree that the Christian religion is, in the long run, a thing of unspeakable comfort. But it does not begin in comfort; it begins in the dismay I have been describing, and it is no use at all trying to go on to that comfort without first going through that dismay. In religion, as in war and everything else, comfort is the one thing you cannot get by looking for it. If you look for truth, you may find comfort in the end; if you look for comfort you will not get either comfort or truth—only soft soap and wishful thinking to begin with and, in the end, despair.*[35]

Put simply, Christianity includes some tenets we struggle to accept, let alone defend. But they are part of a wonderful package.

Fallen

So, does God send people to hell? Does He allow His role as righteous judge to overpower His impulse as loving Father?

In short, no. God doesn't send people to hell. He does something equally disturbing. He leaves it up to us.

God made us free agents. That means we can consciously reject good. Foolish? You bet. But it happens every day.

One need only read as far as the third chapter of the Bible to realize men and women can choose the unencumbered thrill of the plunge over the narrow security of the bridge.

Imagine everything you could ever want being placed before you with the invitation to enjoy it all. You may partake as much, as often, and as long as you like. No limits. No guilt. No calories. The only concession on your part is to stay away from one tree with a particular type of fruit. Anything and everything in the world in exchange for one restriction. Adam and Eve were given that choice.

The forbidden fruit symbolized mankind's freedom to accept or reject God's offer of intimacy. God placed the tree in the garden not to tempt but to testify, a daily reminder to Adam and Eve that they could enjoy God's loving protection or chart their own course. The choice was made clear and the consequences explained.

And the Lord God commanded the man, "You are free to eat from any tree in the garden; but you must not eat from the tree of the knowledge of good and evil, for when you eat of it you will surely die." (Genesis 2:16–17)

So what did Adam do? He took a big bite of the fruit. A mistake? Hardly. He made a deliberate choice to spurn God's offer of protective love, a decision that would determine the course of all human history by planting a seed within each of us that grows into an ugly, strangling weed called rebellion.

I consider myself an optimist who tries to give people the benefit of the doubt. I like to think that most people would submit to the truth if they only understood it. Ignorance or confusion drive poor choices, not premeditated rebellion. If only they were given indisputable evidence and dummy-proof instructions, they would accept God's gracious gift. That is what I would like to think.

Unfortunately, that is not the reality.

Pharaoh saw the miracle of the plagues, yet hardened his heart against the God of Israel.

The children of Israel saw the miracles leading to their freedom from bondage, and then their provision in the wilderness, yet crafted a golden calf to worship instead of their clearly superior God.

Or consider perhaps the most striking case in point: the religious leaders of Jesus' day. Immediately after witnessing some of His most dramatic miracles, they did the last thing you might expect.

> *Then he said to the man, "Stretch out your hand." So he stretched it out and it was completely restored, just as sound as the other. But the Pharisees went out and plotted how they might kill Jesus. (Matthew 12:13–14)*

Rather than fall down on their faces to worship Jesus in awe and reverence for His demonstration of divine power, they plotted his death. When confronted by God's reality face to face, some try to destroy the evidence—something they did in another, even more shocking example as described in the twelfth chapter of John's Gospel.

After Jesus raised Lazarus from the dead, the chief priests made plans to put him back in the grave, because word of the miracle caused many to follow Jesus. Hard as it is to accept, when God makes Himself known in dramatic fashion, some resist Him all the more.

> *Even after Jesus had done all these miraculous signs in their presence, they still would not believe in him. (John 12:37)*

I would like to give people the benefit of the doubt. But some make it very hard to do so.

A devilish deal

Why settle for the mundane when you can easily have excitement? Why work long hours for a paycheck when you can acquire great wealth at the drop of a hat? Why grapple for recognition or influence when fame and power can be handed to you on a silver platter? Why restrict yourself to fidelity when just by asking you can enjoy the uninhibited indulgence of variety? Why accept boring old reality when fantasy offers far more fun?

Such questions have characterized the lure of high living since the beginning of time, and a deal offered by the devil himself in numerous stories, one of the most famous penned by English playwright and Shakespeare contemporary,

Christopher Marlowe, mentioned earlier in chapter 4. *The Tragical History of Doctor Faustus* tells of a man dissatisfied with his lot in life, consumed by lust for power, wealth, and fame. In the words of the play's central protagonist...

Ay, these are those that Faustus most desires.
O, what a world of profit and delight,
Of power, of honour, of omnipotence,
Is promised to the studious artizan![36]

Bored by the tedious yet legitimate disciplines of law, philosophy, theology, and other studies reflecting divine restrictions on human pursuits, Faustus willingly takes a forbidden shortcut to his goals by mastering the dark arts.

A sound magician is a mighty god:
Here, Faustus, tire thy brains to gain a deity!
... Philosophy is odious and obscure;
Both law and physic are for petty wits;
Divinity is basest of the three,
Unpleasant, harsh, contemptible, and vile:
'Tis magic, magic, that hath ravish'd me.[37]

As Faustus pores over his books, a good angel and a demon join the doctor in his study. The former warns that such blasphemous pursuits invite God's wrath. The latter encourages going forward in the dark arts, and learning to control nature's mysterious elements.

Heeding the advice that best quenches his wicked thirst, Faustus conjures up one of hell's servants with a chillingly profane incantation.

Away with the triple deity of Jehovah! Hail, spirits of
fire, air, water and earth! Prince of the East [Lucifer],
Belzebub, monarch of burning hell, and Demogrogon, we
propitiate you, that Mephistophilis may appear and rise.[38]

Mephistophilis emerges at Faustus's request in the garb of a Franciscan friar. Faustus's petition is simple. He asks Mephistophilis to wait upon his every command as would a genie freed from the bottle. Hell's servant must seek permission from the Prince of Darkness before granting such a request.

Faustus: Now tell me what says Lucifer, thy lord?

Meph: That I shall wait on Faustus while he lives, So he
will buy my service with his soul … Thou must bequeath
it solemnly, And write a deed of gift with thine own blood.

So goes the devilish deal. You can have a lifetime of wealth, fame, power, and orgies. But there is one stipulation. They come in exchange for your eternal soul.

Meph: But tell me, Faustus, shall I have thy soul? And
I will be thy slave, and wait on thee, And give thee more
than thou hast wit to ask.

Faustus: Ay, Mephistophilis, I give it thee.[39]

And so, the doctor takes a shortcut to his dreams. But, in the words of Aslan of Narnia, "All get what they want. They do not always like it."

Few literary scenes are as pitiful as the aged Doctor Faustus's mourning the pending torment of his everlasting soul as he takes his final earthly breath. Nor as instructive as the epilogue with Marlowe's grave admonition...

> *Faustus is gone: regard his hellish fall,*
> *Whose fiendful fortune may exhort the wise,*
> *Only to wonder at unlawful things,*
> *Whose deepness doth entice such forward wits*
> *To practise more than heavenly power permits.*[40]

Countless tales echo the theme of Marlowe's famous play, including *The Devil and Daniel Webster* by Stephen Vincent Benét, in which a poor farmer is offered a similar contract. Down on his luck, he sells his immortal soul to the devil for seven years of fortune, concluding with a courtroom battle between the infamous Daniel Webster and the devil himself. The story was put to film in 1941 and again in the 1981 comedic retelling titled *The Devil and Max Devlin*, starring Bill Cosby.

In *The Devil's Advocate*, by Andrew Neiderman, a promising young lawyer is lured by criminal defense attorney John Milton to gain wealth and status by successfully representing the vilest of the vile. As it turns out, John Milton is actually the devil trying to seduce his young protégé into choosing the temporary pleasures of sin over the boring bliss of blessedness.

Yet another variation shows up in Oscar Wilde's *The Picture of Dorian Gray,* the tale of a handsome young playboy who enjoys a reckless, self-destructive lifestyle of pleasure while bearing none of the physical marks of aging and corruption his soul accumulates over time. His face and body remain ever perfect, the deterioration transferred instead to a portrait hidden safely away in his attic. The young man eventually goes mad, killing himself in a fit of well-earned remorse.

Different twists on the same idea: our tendency to choose immediate gratification over long-term joy, and that deep-seated human drive to transcend what ought to be. More than mere literary devices, these themes reflect real choices made by real people who willfully reject God's gracious gifts.

One of my all-time favorite books, titled *The Great Divorce,* tells the story of what happens to a group of hell's inhabitants loaded onto a bus for a day visit to heaven. Most go reluctantly, used to the misery they inhabit. A misery, after all, they have carefully fashioned for some time.

Upon arrival, the visitors complain about the sharp edge of reality that cuts the tender soles of their feet, and how the brightness of true light offends their eyes. Most find the true beauty of heaven's perimeter a disagreeable sight, and wonder why anyone would choose to inhabit such a harsh domain.

As in Dante's epic poem that inspired *The Great Divorce,* the writer is guided through the afterworld by a great poet who explains the dilemma of the damned. One by one, the author and his guide eavesdrop on conversations between the ghostly visitors and those heavenly residents he calls Solid People. You quickly learn of the countless techniques, excuses, and self-deceptions for those desperate to avoid ultimate realities, such as universal truth and selfless love.

The despicable, miserable creatures he observes were not condemned to hell by God's tyrannical rule, but by their own choice.

> *There are only two kinds of people in the end: those who say to God, "Thy will be done," and those to whom God says, in the end, "Thy will be done." All that are in Hell, choose it.*[41]

Again, when we reject the good that God is, we embrace the evil He isn't.

> *There is but one good; that is God. Everything else is good when it looks to Him and bad when it turns from Him. And the higher and mightier it is in the natural order, the more demoniac it will be if it rebels. It's not out of bad mice or bad fleas you make demons, but out of bad archangels.*[42]

The chilling reality is this: since man ranks so high in the created order, we too can become demons... or something worse.

GOING DEEPER

Use the following to prompt further reflection, or to facilitate a group discussion.

Read 2 Peter 2:4–17 and reflect on the following questions.

- Why do you think the rebellious angels and false teachers share a similar fate? What do they have in common?

- The author describes the harshest punishment as "wages of unrighteousness" for those who "cannot cease from sin" and who "[entice] unstable souls" (NKJV). How does this reflect the outworking of free choice rather than punishment from a vindictive God?

Read Revelation 20:11–15 and reflect on the following questions.

- At the conclusion of history, the Bible describes something called a "great white throne" with God opening a "Book of Life" from which people are judged "according to their works" (NKJV). Since those not found in the book are cast into the lake of fire, who is being judged according to works?

- Salvation is a free gift thanks to the sacrifice of Jesus Christ. How, then, do our works in this life impact rewards in the next?

9

One Way
Why So Exclusive?

An assortment of appetizers and desserts crowd the kitchen table. Small paper plates balance on the edge next to a bowl of tortilla-style chips and some specially prepared Mexican bean dip. Wishing I had skipped dinner, I dutifully fill my plate and enter the adjoining living room with the others. The setting looks and feels like a typical small group Bible study: a handful of friendly people enjoying high fat foods and soda while seated in a circle on a long couch and folding chairs. As the only outsider, I can tell the seven regulars feel quite chummy with one another thanks to years of participation in what organizers label a Food for Thought gathering.

I will be interviewing the group, a collection of independent thinkers from various cultural, political, and religious backgrounds who meet monthly to discuss the latest controversy. Earlier topics have included homosexual rights, the place of religion in the public square, and differing opinions on life after death. The city launched these conversation clusters in an effort to foster respect and unity in an otherwise divided town. They figured if those who disagree met to chat over soda and Mexican bean dip every now and then, civility might prevail whenever the city council faced its next polarizing debate. Whether the strategy worked doesn't seem to matter to the seven folks gathered on this evening. They just enjoy one another's diverse company.

And I do mean diverse, something that becomes apparent after asking each person to briefly describe his or her current religious status: two evangelical Christians, one recovering Catholic, and four who could be called "dabblers."

I get the label from Neil when he describes his own religious history.

"I'm not an atheist," he explains. "I was raised Catholic. I don't go to church or practice any particular religion. I don't know how to define myself. I dabble, I guess."

In his late thirties, stocky build with a mild demeanor, Neil looks a bit like the kid in high school everyone liked but who ate lunch alone anyway. Despite regular participation in mass and catechism during childhood, Christianity didn't take.

"When I turned fourteen, my parents gave me a choice, so I left the church. I didn't buy into it, feeling it was just a story. I'm sure there was a bit of kid rebellion mixed in, but the whole thing seemed weird to me. So I rejected it all."

I ask Neil to describe his "dabbling" in more detail.

"I visit the Congregational church downtown once in a while, whenever I hit a rough spot in my life. I've tried a variety of churches, but for some reason I am turned off by those that seem casual and unorganized."

He recalls a few incidents visiting charismatic services.

"Maybe it is a carryover from my Catholic upbringing, but I think to myself, *This isn't a church. This is a 7-Eleven with a clown. They're nuts!*"

I guess Neil feels more comfortable with the sane church he rejected.

Can Neil summarize the basic beliefs of Christianity? He takes a stab.

"I think it is just belief in Jesus Christ and His teachings. I don't know all of what goes into that, but He is at the center."

Next to Neil sits Donna who describes herself as "An unaffiliated, sort-of Christian. Whatever that means." Her tense laughter suggests embarrassment: perhaps worried such a vague description seems unrefined. I get the impression that Donna, a fifty-something wife and mother, enjoys hanging around sophisticated people who prop up her hesitant confidence, and that she works very hard to avoid appearing insecure.

"I believe in God, Jesus, and the Bible as a source of truth, but not the final source. When I do attend church, which isn't often, I go to the Unitarian church. A fringe Christian might be a good description."

I suppose you could call Donna a second generation "fringe believer" since her father, raised Catholic, married her German Lutheran mother. Rather than choose between the two denominations, they "did a little bit of nothing" with the kids, making hers a non-religious upbringing. Donna married a man who grew up in and was turned off by the Baptist church, so they followed in her parent's footsteps and did nothing religious with their children beyond Christmas and Easter church services.

"We did teach them the golden rule and in the existence of a higher being," she quickly and defensively adds. "I believe I have a great deal of spirituality. But to me it does not require church on an every-Sunday basis to have a good relationship with God."

"You're a lapsed dabbler?" someone asks with a laugh.

The rest of the group chuckles at the label. And since she figures they are laughing with her rather than at her, Donna joins in with a big smile.

As with Neil, I ask Donna for a summary of the basics of Christian belief.

"As I understand it," she strains, "Jesus Christ is the Son of God, sent to earth to teach us how to live and how to die. He died and was resurrected so that we could all have life everlasting."

Pretty good for a lapsed dabbler.

Moving around the room we come to Wade, a fiftyish guy with black hair and dark complexion suggesting an unidentifiably mixed racial heritage, possibly including Native American. I have a hard time following Wade, in part because he mumbles softly, forcing me to strain and repeat my requests in order to catch what he says. But also because he seems intent on avoiding any sort of label or pre-defined box for his religious orientation. He doesn't like me asking about his current religious status.

"Are you talking religious or spiritual?" he asks.

I've always disliked it when people force that distinction, such as when believers say things such as "I am talking about relationship, not religion." I understand and agree with their point. But the separation feels unnecessarily forced.

"Both or either," I respond, avoiding his trap.

"I believe I am progressing and I've always been a spiritually sensitive person," Wade begins.

I wonder to myself whether "spiritually sensitive" means a sensitive heart, or something more like a sensitive tooth. Does his story hide deep pain?

"I am a searcher and a seeker of the truth. I receive spirituality in many ways. I believe that all religions have a piece of the truth, and that all deviate a little bit."

Moving from the present to childhood, I learn that Wade has indeed experienced the sensitive tooth of religious abuse. His family was deeply entrenched in the Worldwide Church of God: a highly control-oriented cult led by Herbert W. Armstrong, someone I vaguely recall setting and missing the date of Jesus' return during the 1970s. I've met others from that movement, and I see the same look in Wade's eyes: like a cowering, abused puppy who would get defiant if he weren't so afraid of the next slap.

"It is a difficult thing to leave a cult," Wade continues. "Most people have no idea… "

His voice trails off as if the unpleasant memories make it impossible for him to continue this line of thought. He hits fast forward, moving to the next significant scene in his spiritual journey.

"During my late teens, after leaving the Worldwide Church, I got into meditation. I am still searching and seeking. Because of those early experiences I am not open to the structure of religion."

As I piece together bits of mumbled phrases, Wade's experience begins to take shape. After leaving his parents' cult, he spent three decades avoiding formal religion. He gravitated toward mystical, quasi-pantheistic spirituality mixed with skepticism. Wade took pride in his tendency to question the motives of anyone considered a religious leader.

"What I love is what we are doing now," he smiles, "sitting around, informally discussing spiritual matters. I love the genuine. I love the sincere. It's got to be the real thing."

Asked for his summary of basic Christianity, Wade becomes clearly uncomfortable. I remember that he dislikes boxes. "The definition of Christianity is complete love," he reluctantly offers. "It is to have the entire God living in you."

I try pinning Wade down to something more precise to no avail. He seems content with his inability to clearly explain, somehow taking comfort in ambiguity and the eternal "searching and seeking" it allows.

At last I come to Sarah, our host for the evening. A glance at the wall decorations and bookshelf selections suggests that Sarah favors some sort of eastern religion, perhaps Hindu or Buddhist. Her physical appearance reinforces the notion: a slight frame, she looks like a former flower child who now eats nothing but organically grown bird food.

"I guess, like Neil, I'd call myself a dabbler," Sarah begins.

"I don't really believe in God, but I believe in the idea of God. And I can see why people believe, because it would be nice to have a faith. But I don't."

I feel surprised that one who believes only in the idea rather than the reality of God surrounds herself with so many religiously oriented paintings and books. The rest of her story helps fill in the blanks. Raised a very staid and stoic Episcopalian, Sarah retains a level of respect for her parents' beliefs.

"Both of my parents are people who I think of as truly religious, in that what they do and how they treat other people has a religious basis. One of the reasons I have some good feelings about Christianity is I see how generous and kind and thoughtful my parents are."

Sarah loves the church her folks currently attend because, unlike so many others, "it welcomes anyone and everyone." Code language for ordaining gay priests and blessing homosexual unions.

"If there is such a thing as being a true Christian, I'd say my parents are," she continues. "But I think that other religions embody that same idea of treating others the way you'd like to be treated yourself."

Out of the corner of my eye I catch Donna nodding in recognition of the "golden rule" she taught her kids.

"I've also had some influence from eastern religions that have been really positive," Sarah explains. After college she went to Nepal with the Peace Corps where she lived within and among Hindu and Buddhist cultures. She never formally studied the teachings of either, but still found herself impressed by belief systems that felt less rigid and structured: more organic to daily life.

"I enjoyed the experience of living among those for whom these belief systems were simply part of the fabric of their society. Many were Hindu and Buddhist at the same time without seeing a conflict," she explains.

Sarah considers the Dalai Lama her hero because he seems to live a peaceful lifestyle. And yet, she never formally became Buddhist.

She also admires one of my favorite Christian writers, and has read quite a bit of his writings. Maybe that is part of the reason Sarah retains a residue of goodwill for Christianity.

"I'm really conflicted," she says. "In many ways, I have somewhat a positive feeling toward Christianity. I light candles for friends who have died. I love the ritual and ceremony associated with religion. There have been times in my life when I have prayed, and hoped that it went somewhere."

Curious about what might have pushed Sarah away from the faith for which she retains so much goodwill, I uncover the usual suspect: a college philosophy class that, in her words, "made me think a lot about belief, existentialism, atheism, Christianity, history, and how they are all interrelated." In other words, she had a biased professor, evidenced by her recap of history as "a series of atrocities carried out in the name of religions like Christianity."

"I know it sounds naïve to say so," Sarah admits, "but it is hard for me to understand how people who believe in God could do such things."

How does Sarah define Christianity? A long pause suggesting serious contemplation precedes a reference to something a believing cousin shared with her.

"He said that Christianity is the only religion that has complete forgiveness as one of its main tenets."

A good summary, but one Sarah doesn't buy.

"I'm not sure I agree with that, but it is one of the things that people say defines Christianity."

Almost as an afterthought, she adds a few more defining tenets.

"There is also the Holy Trinity of Father, Son and Holy Ghost, that somehow the three entities are one-in-the-same in sort of an odd way. There is life after death, which is not only in Christianity but is, I think, an important part of it."

"Anything specific about Jesus?" I ask.

"Yes, that He actually died for our sins and then came back to life."

Clearly, some of her church lessons stuck. So, where did such an eclectic history leave Sarah?

"I would personally like to think that the Muslim God, the Hindu God, the Buddhist God, and the Christian God are the same God."

"Is that what you would like to think, or what you do think?" I prod.

"Well, as I said, I don't really believe in God. But I think the God that people create spiritually, if there is one, is the same."

I pose one final question to the group.

"How do you explain the fact that others fully embrace Christian belief, while you don't? I have spoken to folks with stories and experiences remarkably similar to those you've shared tonight, who believe. Why do you think they accept what you reject?"

"The Lord works in mysterious ways," Donna takes a stab. "God exists in all of us, pursues all of us differently, asks us all to follow Him differently because we all have different paths to pursue. Some people have questioning to do in different ways. We all have our works to do, and God has set up differently how He has us do them. Some choose to be born-again Christians to know God. Others choose to know God in other ways."

According to Donna, who believes in many ways to God, it is His plan for us to choose divergent paths.

Sarah hesitantly offers a different viewpoint. "I think in some ways it is easier to believe than not believe. I would really like to believe, because I think it would be comforting."

In other words, those who believe do so for the same reason my daughter sleeps with a teddy bear: it just feels better.

Finally, Neil haltingly offers an explanation that he admits could make him sound like a jerk. "What makes me different from those who believe is that they are able to suspend some of their questions, or suspend reality, and just say they believe by faith. But I feel like I just can't stop asking questions, and the answers I get just don't satisfy. I don't think I'm smarter or anything like that. It's just that I feel there are a lot of questions that aren't answered, and maybe someone who believes can just take it on faith."

"What a jerk!" someone jokingly jibes.

But I appreciate Neil's honesty. His questions haven't been answered to his satisfaction, making it difficult for him to take the faith leap. Of course, as you might expect from the lead dabbler, he doesn't seem serious about pursuing those answers.

As I finish my list of questions, I glance down and notice that I have taken only one bite of each selection scooped onto my plate. I had spent the evening merely playing with my food to keep up appearances. I consider myself in good company: a group of dabblers spending their lives nibbling around the edges of spirituality without ever really digging in.

Smorgasbord

My visit with the Food for Thought group reminds me of a *Life* magazine cover story from several years earlier in which a photo-laced essay summarized the many views of God found in some of the major and minor religious movements of America. From solemn women in a Salt Lake City tabernacle, to prostrate men facing Mecca as they pray, to smiling singers at a Billy Graham crusade, the author portrays some of the largest faith groups of our culture, including Catholics, Protestants, evangelicals, Mormons, and Jews. He also highlights less visible but growing sects such as Hindus, Buddhists, and Holy Rollers, as well as Greek and Russian Orthodox believers.

The feature writer was Frank McCourt, a lapsed Catholic who became the wildly successful author of the book *Angela's*

Ashes. His final paragraph summarized well the perspective of many in this generation.

> *I don't confine myself to the faith of my fathers anymore.*
> *All the religions are spread before me, a great spiritual*
> *smorgasbord, and I'll help myself, thank you.*[43]

Like all dabblers, McCourt will pick and choose the portions of various faiths that he likes, leaving behind those he doesn't.

Jeremiah Creedon seconds the motion. He wrote a story titled "Designer God" for a leading alternative media magazine, in which he posed the telling question, "In a mix-and-match world, why not create your own religion?" Creedon suggests we embrace what has been labeled "cafeteria religion" as a new approach to faith and the truest spiritual quest of all. The opening paragraph says it all.

> *A friend of mine I'll call Anne-Marie is the founder of a*
> *new religious faith. Like other belief systems throughout*
> *the ages, the sect of Anne-Marie exists to address life's*
> *most haunting questions. If I ask her why we're born and*
> *what happens when we die, her answers suggest that*
> *our time on earth has meaning and purpose. Whether*
> *I buy it hardly matters. The sect of Anne-Marie has one*
> *member, Anne-Marie, and that's plenty.*[44]

Such a "mix-and-match" approach to faith has its own story. The CliffsNotes version reads something like, "There is no big story. There is only whatever fable you can piece together from the seemingly random experiences of life."

It is like taking ten novels, each with different characters and plots, and ripping chapter one from the first book, chapter two from the second and so on. Hoping to enjoy a new story by reading the excised chapters in sequence, you instead find nonsense and confusion. Rather than experiencing each religious story as written, we have ripped random scenes from various subplots in hopes of creating our own scripts.

But it hasn't worked. And many are facing the harsh reality that treating truth claims as "a great spiritual smorgasbord" from which to "help myself, thank you" is another way of saying none of them are true in an ultimate sense.

Another famous writer, Douglas Coupland, coined the term *Generation X* in the title of an earlier best-seller while giving voice to the angst of an entire generation, those whose youth was stained with scenes of the Kennedy and King assassinations, the Vietnam conflict, Watergate, gas lines, and the Iran hostage crisis. In his most disturbing novel, aptly titled *Life After God*, Coupland tells the story of a young man wandering from one empty experience to the next in search of meaning or purpose in his life: a man who yearns to run so that his spirit can feel the brisk breeze of joy, beauty, clarity, and vitality. But instead he drags a heavy ball of unbelief affixed during childhood. "I was wondering what was the logical end product of this recent business of my feeling less and less," Coupland's character reflects in response to the soul-numbing routine of daily existence.

"Is feeling nothing the inevitable end result of believing in nothing? And then I got to feeling frightened—thinking that there might not actually be anything to believe in, in particular. I thought it would be such a sick joke to have to remain alive for decades and not believe in or feel anything."[45]

This shoot of unbelief sprouted from a very specific root: parents who raised their son without religion because they had broken with their own pasts. Having escaped the rigors of Christian commitment, they set their children free. But unbelief, according to one immersed in its hardening mud, does not free. It entombs. It cuts us off from the cool refreshment of clear direction. It places us on the rat's treadmill rather than the runner's path. Perhaps worst of all, it makes the inviting notion of sincere belief something beyond comprehension, an internal conflict Douglas Coupland captures in his protagonist's description of Christian media.

And there were Christian radio stations, too, so many many stations, and the voices on them seemed so enthusiastic and committed. They sounded like they sincerely believed in what they were saying, and so for once I decided to pay attention to these stations, trying to figure out what exactly it was they were believing in, trying to understand the notion of Belief...

The radio stations all seemed to be talking about Jesus nonstop, and it seemed to be this crazy orgy

*of projection, with everyone projecting onto Jesus
the antidotes to the things that had gone wrong in
their own lives. He is Love. He is Forgiveness. He is
Compassion. He is a Wise Career Decision. He is a
Child Who Loves Me.*

*I was feeling a sense of loss as I heard these people.
I felt like Jesus was sex—or rather, I felt like I was from
another world where sex did not exist and I arrived
on Earth and everyone talked about how good sex felt,
and showed me their pornography and built their lives
around sex, and yet I was forever cut off from the true
sexual experience. I did not deny that the existence of
Jesus was real to these people—it was merely that I was
cut off from their experience in a way that was never
connectable.*[46]

It is one thing to reject Christianity because you don't
understand it. It is another to do so because you can't
comprehend the experience of real belief, something made
more difficult when parents leave you to decide for yourself
among religious options so varied that claiming certainty
seems naïvely arrogant or even dangerous.

Narrowing the options

I sympathize with the frustration over what seems an endless
line of religious perspectives. But there really are not as many
as most people think. The modern trend toward relativism has

made us lazy by suggesting there are far too many irreconcilable belief systems out there for anyone to compare and contrast. We throw up our hands and either embrace the one most convenient, or reject them all.

But it need not be so complicated. Put simply, every worldview story grows out of some view of God. There are only three options in response to the question—Does God exist? Those who say "no" are atheists. Those who say "yes" are theists. Those who say "nobody knows" are agnostics.

The atheist, for example, lives in a story that goes something like this…

> *Once upon a time there was matter. Through a random series of accidents, this matter evolved into life. There is nothing beyond the material universe, and we can know nothing beyond what we grasp using our five senses. The world is a big entertainment complex that is closing soon. So have a good time while you can. And good luck— you'll need it!*

This "plot" encourages us to grab all the gusto we can while we can because when it's over, it's over. That may seem overly simplistic, but what other story can be told? Without an author—there can be no larger purpose to the scenes of our lives.

If you believe that God exists, you can either believe there is one God (monotheism) or more than one God (polytheism). A dominant worldview during the ancient days of the Greek and Roman empires, there are relatively few polytheist faiths in the West beyond Mormonism.

If there is one God, He is either a personal being who created everything (a view embraced by the three primary religions of the world—Christianity, Judaism, and Islam), or an impersonal force of which we are part (a view represented by eastern pantheism and its new age variations).

If you believe in a personal God, you must ask yourself a few questions that sort through the various world religions. For example, does He demand that we do the work to get to Him, or does He do the work in pursuit of us? Do we earn God's favor, or does God win our hearts? It is the answer to these questions that makes the Christian faith unique. It teaches that God pursues man, trying to set him free. In every other religion, man pursues God, trying to redeem himself. Those stories might read something like this...

Once upon a time, God made people. He wanted them to behave themselves, but they didn't. In fact, they messed up pretty bad. So God gave them a list of things to do in order to get back into his good graces. From religious ceremonies to strict rules and regulations, God spelled out everything people needed to do in order to fix the problems they caused. And He is still waiting for them to get their act together.

There will always be another prayer to pray, deed to perform, sin to confess, or service to attend. If we are honest, we all know we can never measure up. So we either give up entirely, or develop ulcers trying.

Again, there are other stories being told. Each has a different plot and claims to be the one true drama. But only one has the amazing scene in which the Author decides to lay aside His pen, enter the story, and play the Hero. The gospel is the one plot where God redeems man rather than man tries to redeem himself.

Open-minded

Prior to 10 May 1985, I thought of myself as a fairly open-minded guy. Since then I have become narrow-minded and biased, limiting myself to one possibility out of many. You see, on that day, I got married. And saying "I do" to one woman meant saying "I don't" to the rest. That doesn't mean I hate all other women. But it does mean they ceased to be options for me.

The same thing happened when I embraced Christianity. Accepting one belief meant rejecting others. When we pick and choose from various religious traditions, we do not show our broad-mindedness or inclusivity. We are more like the man who sleeps with multiple women. He doesn't take sexual intimacy seriously. Rather than sacred, he sees sex as a game.

Religion is like marriage. It is by definition exclusive. That doesn't mean a religious person hates all other faiths, or even views them as entirely wrong. But we can't view them as equally right. The creed of each excludes the creed of others. Jesus certainly did so when He rejected the notion that all paths lead to God.

Enter through the narrow gate. For wide is the gate and broad is the road that leads to destruction, and many enter through it. But small is the gate and narrow the road that leads to life, and only a few find it. (Matthew 7:13–14)

Jesus clearly claimed exclusivity.

I am the way and the truth and the life. No-one comes to the Father except through me. (John 14:6)

But Jesus also made His offer available to everyone…

For God so loved the world that he gave his one and only Son, that whoever believes in him shall not perish but have eternal life. For God did not send his Son into the world to condemn the world, but to save the world through him. (John 3:16–17)

I believe every person is on a spiritual journey, seeking the truth. But for some, the journey seems more like aimless wandering: never quite reaching the intended destination. Every quest should have a prize. Every search is supposed to find. While I believe all religions reach for the same God, Jesus said they don't all find Him. On one level, I don't want to hear that. On another level, I know it's true. It *must* be. If we believe in everything, we believe in nothing. Jesus is either who He claimed or He's an arrogant liar. He died paying for my sins, or He died getting what He deserved. As a Christian, I believe

Jesus' claim to be the intended destination of every spiritual quest. He is the prize pursued, the truth sought.

In short, the best reason to embrace Christianity is, in the words of G. K. Chesterton,

> *because it fits the lock; because it is like life. It is one*
> *among many stories; only it happens to be a true story.*
> *It is one among many philosophies; only it happens to be*
> *the truth. We accept it; and the ground is solid under our*
> *feet and the road is open before us.*[47]

The road is open before us. Christians do not need to live a closed-minded life. God may not be in all things, but He can and does speak through all things. The atheist has to see most of the world as mad or delusional. The Christian, on the other hand, is free to hold a more liberal view, to see others as partly right because they've picked up bits and pieces of truth that resonate with the heart while pointing them to the one, true God who is revealing Himself to everyone: believers and dabblers alike.

Finding our place

In the now ancient 1987 film based upon an autobiographical book by Shirley MacLaine, titled *Out on a Limb*, one scene depicts pantheistic understanding in a manner most viewers found troubling. MacLaine stands on the beach beside David, her spiritual mentor, who invites her to repeat several short phrases. Normally, the ocean makes us feel humbled and small, recognizing how great our Creator must be. But David doesn't coach her to shout "Great is the Lord" or "How wonderful is your handiwork" to the God of heaven. He instead asks her to repeat three simple words: "I am God!" MacLaine hesitates. "David, I can't do that." To which he responds, "See how little you think of yourself?"

With a little coaxing she agrees to do as instructed, timidly at first. But as they repeat the phrase over and over in unison her conviction grows. They turn toward the ocean, its crashing waves echoing its size and majesty, and continue their mantra: "I am God! I am God!"[48]

To someone like me, the scene shouts ultimate arrogance and blasphemy. But to MacLaine and others who embrace pantheism, it reveals the ultimate discovery. Shirley had finally come to realize her "true" identity. She believed she was part of God. Her drop of water had finally accepted its place in the vast ocean of our collective godhood.

I find it interesting that even those who claim to be God expect Him to be more. Shirley MacLaine shouted in front of mighty waves, not a trickling faucet. Her drop, like mine, longs for the ocean. And we both hope God is infinitely greater than ourselves.

We all yearn to be put in our place so that we know we have one. Despite our protests to the contrary, we need a God who is more than we want Him to be. A God who is perfect love, strict father, divine comedian, blinding light, first cause, jealous husband, uncensored truth, eternal wrath, omniscient author, even the one and only way.

A God who is, in short, an awful goodness.

GOING DEEPER

Use the following to prompt further reflection, or to facilitate a group discussion.

Read about Paul's encounter with the eclectic religious culture of his day in Acts 17:16–34, and then reflect on the following questions.

- What can we learn from Paul's approach to the pluralistic religious culture of his day?

- In light of Paul's approach, how might we respect a variety of religious perspectives without treating them all as equally valid?

10

Omniscient Author
God Writes the Story

In what became the most popular fantasy of the twentieth century, J. R. R. Tolkien's *The Lord of the Rings* tells the epic tale of two ordinary hobbits who find themselves central characters on an extraordinary adventure. Threatened by the terror of an evil ruler, young Frodo and Sam flee the quiet Shire of their home with a company of brave companions on a quest to keep the Ring of Doom from the forces of darkness. After a particularly frightening encounter, the two are separated from the security of the larger group, requiring Frodo and Sam to press on alone if there is to be any hope of success. To do so, they must push through their fears, and confront unknown dangers and horrors darker than any nightmare. But unlike those who remained in the safety of the Shire, Frodo and Sam see their lives as part of something more important than personal comfort and security. They see themselves serving a plot much bigger than their own. And so, risking everything, they continue their quest against overwhelming odds.

At several points along their journey, Frodo and Sam gain strength and perspective by reflecting upon what happens in the stories that really matter, comparing them to the tale in which they find themselves. Hardly a quest they would have willingly pursued, it is, nevertheless, one they must continue. As Sam suggests, in the best tales people encounter dangerous risks, and despite lots of chances to do so, they refuse to turn back. "And if they had, we shouldn't know, because they'd have been forgotten." Some heroes go on to face peril rather than a good end. At least, as Sam puts it, "not to what folk inside a story call a good end." That is the catch. Those living in the story would prefer to be kept safe rather than risk danger.

> "But those aren't always the best tales to hear, though they may be the best tales to get landed in! I wonder what sort of a tale we've fallen into?"
>
> "I wonder," said Frodo. "But I don't know. And that's the way of a real tale. Take any one that you're fond of. You may know, or guess, what kind of a tale it is, happy-ending or sad-ending, but the people in it don't know. And you don't want them to."[49]

Sam and Frodo, placed in a tale filled with uncertainty, knew that the stakes were high. They knew theirs was an important role. But they didn't know how it would end. And we don't want them to. That would take all suspense and mystery out of the story.

I draw inspiration by the reflections of two little hobbits. First, like Sam and Frodo, I am in the midst of a tale filled with uncertainty. I know that the stakes are high, and that mine is an important role. But I don't know how it will end. And I shouldn't know, lest the mystery be lost. I often find myself upset that the script of my life has not turned out as planned. But then again, maybe it has. Maybe the circumstances I least like are those most important to the story being told. Perhaps the Author has written me into a script that is about something bigger than my personal comfort and security. Leaving me to wonder: what sort of tale have I fallen into?

Tolkien's heroes taught me a second lesson. Sam and Frodo recognized that their part, while pivotal to the larger drama, was still just a part. Reflecting upon their adventure, Sam's excitement is tempered by sober speculation.

> *"What a tale we have been in, Mr. Frodo, haven't we?"*
> *he said. "I wish I could hear it told! … And I wonder*
> *how it will go on after our part."*[50]

They knew that the story would go on without them. Their quest, no matter how remarkable, was not the main plot. Their lives, as wonderful as they may be, were only subplots of a much bigger drama. This realization connected Sam and Frodo to something greater than themselves—a transcendent reality that inspires heroic self-sacrifice rather than cowardly self-preservation. That something greater enabled Frodo to say at the end of his quest…

> *"I have been deeply hurt, Sam. I tried to save the Shire,*
> *and it has been saved, but not for me. It must often be*
> *so, Sam, when things are in danger: some one has to give*
> *them up, lose them, so that others may keep them."*[51]

My life is not the main plot of reality. When self-centered pride convinces me otherwise, my story becomes the timid and passionless pursuit of safety and comfort. The humble spirit, on the other hand, submits itself to a larger, transcendent story: turning life into a passionate adventure filled with purpose. Pride creates cowards. Humility inspires heroes. Leaving me to wonder—what heroic purpose was I made to serve?

The questions raised during my encounter with Frodo and Sam evoke other, more challenging questions. My theology tells me there is indeed an author to the epic story of history and the scenes in which I play my part. The yearnings of my heart tell me there is more going on than what I see, calling me to a purpose beyond my own gratification—to something heroic. But when and how does the inspiring promise of a grand drama touch the trying reality of the daily grind? It is easy to see yourself part of an epic drama while in a fantastic adventure saving the world from the clutches of evil. It becomes more difficult amid difficult circumstances with no clear resolution, or when facing yet another day of incessant boredom. Few of us reside in a life story filled with endless excitement and amazement. Stuck in the tedious and sometimes painful experiences of life, many of us wonder where it is, exactly, that life and story meet.

Is life part of story when the baby's diaper needs changing for the sixth time today? What about when the paycheck is $200 short of the bills, or the doctor recommends a few more tests to "eliminate certain possibilities." Where is "happily ever after" when a husband walks out the door after twenty years of marriage to chase a younger skirt, or an angry child leaves home screaming "I hate you" to his heartbroken parents? Such real-life scenes sometimes cause us to wonder whether life and story meet at all.

But they do. And how we respond in the most trying moments plays a major part in how the story of our lives will be told.

Such a time

An orphan raised by relatives, she didn't have what you would call a normal, happy childhood. Barely beyond puberty, she was suddenly taken away to gratify the sexual desires of a harsh, arrogant man. Her beauty drove him wild, and he used her body to fulfill his passions whenever he was in the mood. The rest of the time he found little use for her—so she spent most of her time waiting to be summoned along with the other girls whose only earthly purpose was to satisfy his lusts. Miserable life circumstances, to be sure. But it was precisely these unhappy scenes that enabled Esther to play a key part in one of the most exciting subplots ever performed.

During a banquet thrown for his government officials and military officers, an intoxicated King Xerxes thought it would be fun to give the guys a few thrills by having a girl jump out of a cake. His wife, Queen Vashti, was the obvious choice. After all, she was a knockout—and he was proud to show off her beauty. There was just one problem. Vashti didn't like the idea, and refused to come. The king was furious. So, like any good husband, he disowned her and commanded her to stay out of his sight forever.

Thus launched the search for the new Mrs. Xerxes. The king's attendants proposed a search to assemble the most beautiful young virgins of the empire into a royal harem. And so, just like that, every pretty girl in the kingdom of Xerxes was at risk of becoming part of his personal Playboy Bunny collection. Each would spend months going through a special beauty treatment and diet regimen before modeling her stuff in front of an eager king. Eventually, one of them would be given the "honor" of replacing Vashti as queen and future stag party entertainment. That one, as the story would have it, was a young Jewish girl named Esther.

> *Now the king was attracted to Esther more than to any of the other women, and she won his favor and approval more than any of the other virgins. So he set a royal crown on her head and made her queen instead of Vashti … But Esther had kept secret her family background and nationality. (Esther 2:17, 20 NIV 2011)*

A music bridge takes us to the next scene…

Having overheard talk of an assassination plot against the king, Esther's uncle Mordecai warns his niece so she can report the conspiracy to the king. The seemingly insignificant detail is briefly noted in the minutes for future posterity, and quickly forgotten.

A sinister-sounding melody takes us to another scene…

After years clawing his way to the top, Haman is finally appointed the king's chief of staff. All other officials are now under his thumb, and every citizen must bow to his greatness. But one person refuses—Mordecai. Infuriated, Haman declares he will not tolerate such insolence. Anti-Semitic to the core, rather than merely punish Mordecai, Haman uses the occasion as an excuse to kill every Jew in the kingdom.

> *Then Haman said to King Xerxes, "There is a certain people dispersed and scattered among the peoples in all the provinces of your kingdom whose customs are different from those of all other people and who do not obey the king's laws; it is not in the king's best interest to tolerate them. If it pleases the king, let a decree be issued to destroy them … (Esther 3:8–9)*

Too busy to be bothered with such petty matters as genocide, the king quickly grants Haman the authority needed to carry out his evil plan. So, a bounty is placed on the head of every Jewish man, woman, and child in the empire.

Meanwhile, back in the palace…

Hearing about the impending murder of her people, Queen Esther is met with the difficult choice between speaking up on behalf of the Jews and quietly preserving her own life. On penalty of death, she is not allowed to enter the king's presence unless summoned. If she simply remains silent, she is safe. But if she approaches the king to plead for intervention, he may order her death along with the masses. Faced with her moment of truth, a frightened young girl seeks advice from the man who raised her.

> *"Do not think that because you are in the king's house you alone of all the Jews will escape. For if you remain silent at this time, relief and deliverance for the Jews will arise from another place, but you and your father's family will perish. And who knows but that you have come to royal position for such a time as this?"* (Esther 4:13–14)

Don't miss the significance of those words. Esther is not advised to intervene because it is their only hope of rescue. He says, "if you remain silent at this time, relief and deliverance for the Jews will arise from another place…" Mordecai knew that the main plot of the grand drama involves the Jewish people—so genocide was impossible. God would intervene another way if necessary. The key is not what will happen in the larger story, but whether or not Esther will play the part she has been chosen to play and fill the role she was destined to fill. "And who knows but that you have come to royal position for such a time as this?"

Like Frodo and Sam, Esther has been given a part in a great drama in order to fulfill a heroic purpose. If she turns back from her quest, the story will go on without her. But Esther will be forgotten. Mordecai is not calling her to save the day, but to fulfill a destiny. The purpose of all of the bad she endured earlier in life suddenly made sense. Esther was placed in the story as queen in order to star in one of the greatest plays ever performed on the stage of history.

Inspired by her uncle's admonition, Esther did risk her life to save others. Seeing her life as part of a story bigger than her own comfort and security gave confidence to face whatever end lay before her.

> *"Go, gather together all the Jews who are in Susa, and fast for me. Do not eat or drink for three days, night or day. I and my maids will fast as you do. When this is done, I will go to the king, even though it is against the law. And if I perish, I perish." (Esther 4:15–16)*

And as for the rest of the story…

Esther did go to the king, and she survived. In fact, Xerxes agreed to grant her any request. Haman built a 75-foot gallows for hanging Mordecai. But the night before the execution, a bad case of insomnia kept the king from sleeping. So he ordered the royal minutes read—including the section describing Mordecai's efforts to uncover the assassination plot. The next day, the story turns with a dramatic flair more entertaining than anything even Shakespeare could conceive.

Mordecai is not hanged, but honored.

Haman is not honored, but hanged on the very gallows he built for Mordecai.

The Jews are not exterminated, but empowered to defend themselves from any attack.

And to this day the celebration of Purim continues to remember the intervention of a young, pretty girl who played a part in the story she would have never chosen, but that she acted to perfection.

Our part

God wants to tell a story through your life and mine. Someday, when the curtain is closed and we leave the stage of time, how our stories fit into the entire drama will become clear. Meanwhile, in His grace, the Author has recorded earlier scenes for our inspiration and instruction. Each is unique, containing its own suspense and mystery. But, in certain ways, they are all the same. All remind us that every detail, no matter how unpleasant or seemingly insignificant, is filled with meaning for the story.

I have often wondered how the drama would change had certain scenes been written to suit the character's desires rather than the story's purpose. In the story of Esther, for example, what would have happened had King Xerxes selected his wife based upon personality and character rather than base lust? Would the beautiful Esther have become queen? Would she have saved the Jews from genocide? Certainly, the Author could have accomplished His purpose by ending Haman's plot in less dramatic form. But He had a story to tell and Esther had a heroic purpose to fulfill.

What if there had never been any sibling rivalry among Jacob's children? After all, the tension between Joseph and his brothers caused him to be thrown down a well, sold into slavery, and condemned to prison. Hardly a part Joseph would have chosen. But it allowed his life to fulfill a great destiny and tell a great story.

What if there had been no decree by Pharaoh to kill innocent Jewish babies in Egypt? Moses would never have been placed on the Nile river in a basket. If he hadn't been on the river he wouldn't have been found by the princess and raised in Pharaoh's household, the precise preparation needed to play the role of deliverer for God's people. Was Pharaoh wrong for what he did? Of course. The schemes of every villain are evil. But God used his sin as a means of orchestrating Moses' destiny and telling an incredible story.

There are countless examples of times God has used negative situations in order to fulfill His purposes with great dramatic impact. None of the men and women inside the story may have liked the role they were chosen to play. But by remaining faithful amid some of the worst circumstances imaginable, they were able to play the part of hero rather than victim. Each was chosen for "such a time" as the drama required. Each did what needed to be done. And in the process each found the sometimes-unhappy place where life and story meet.

When the mundane or painful realities of life are understood to be scenes in the larger drama, they are infused with new meaning and our response with greater import. We are no longer simply changing a diaper, but sacrificing our own enjoyment for the sake of one unable to care for herself. It is in such thankless moments that our lives touch the drama by embracing the role of selfless hero rather than selfish coward.

When the paycheck is short of the bills and we have no idea how we will make ends meet, will we play the role of panicked victim or determined protagonist?

Will the abandoned spouse respond as a devastated outcast or courageously cling to the hand of her true beloved, remaining faithful in the midst of unfaithfulness?

Can a heartbroken parent resist the overwhelming urge to strike back and show love amid rebellion?

When encountering the prospect of death by cancer, can we face the ultimate human enemy without sinking into despair? Can we bravely face its cold, cruel stare with head high, knowing that our story does not end with physical death?

Life and story meet in these most unexpected places. And, just as we do not know how our part fits into the larger drama, we don't know how our responses impact the story being told. But one thing is certain. They do. And some day, when the whole story is told, we will see how.

Most unfortunate

Though only a child, Shasta had lived a miserable life. Raised by a cruel fisherman posing as his father, Shasta discovered that he was actually an orphan only upon overhearing the fisherman trying to sell his "son" to an even worse master. But he escaped with the help of a talking horse named Bree, and headed north to seek freedom in the great land of Narnia. So begins the adventure of *The Horse and His Boy*.[52]

After being frightened by a lion along their journey northward, Shasta and the noble warhorse encounter two other traveling companions who are also trying to reach Narnia—a girl named Aravis, and her filly named Hwin. Along the way, the four face many dangers—including several frightful lion encounters. Eventually, Shasta is separated from the group and forced to press on alone. Finally, he has had enough. Alone and scared, he reflects upon his misery.

He considers himself the most unlucky boy that ever lived, because everything goes right for everyone except for him. Recounting his various trials and misfortunes, Shasta weeps—realizing he is lost, cold, and hungry. Just then, a noise is heard in the brush that frightens the boy, and he asks who is there. The majestic reply is, One who has long waited for him.

Unable to see anyone, wondering if he has encountered a mountain giant or ghoul, Shasta's wavering voice pleads with the mysterious voice to go away and leave him alone. He cries that he is the most unfortunate person in the world.

But then, the soothing breath of the great Aslan overtakes the scene, and the lion king invites Shasta to share his sorrows. Shasta lists his complaints:

- no better than an orphan;

- never knew his real parents;

- raised by a cruel fisherman;

- chased by lions.

Aslan replies that he does not call Shasta unfortunate.

But what about all his troubles? It was certainly bad luck to be chased by so many lions...

Aslan tells him he only met one lion, but that he was swift. Shasta asks how he knows that.

That's when Shasta's frightened eyes finally open to the real story behind his miserable tale.

> "I was the lion who forced you to join with Aravis. I was
> the cat who comforted you among the tombs. I was the
> lion who drove the jackals from you while you slept. I
> was the lion who gave the Horses the new strength of
> fear for the last mile so that you should reach King Lune
> in time. And I was the lion you do not remember who
> pushed the boat in which you lay, a child near death,
> so that it came to shore where a man sat, wakeful at
> midnight, to receive you."[53]

At that moment, Shasta's self-pity and fear dissolve into the realization that the moments of his life he most despised were the very ones being orchestrated by the great king to accomplish a greater purpose, and tell a greater tale.

Like Shasta, we will someday meet the great King and Author of history. Only then will our eyes be opened to the moments in which he was "the lion" orchestrating events toward a greater purpose. Finally, we will better understand how and where life and story met, including the points at which the grand drama of providence intersected the smaller scenes of our lives. I can hardly wait for that moment. Meanwhile, it is enough to know I am called to play my part in the story.

> *In him we were also chosen, having been predestined according to the plan of him who works out everything in conformity with the purpose of his will, in order that we, who were the first to hope in Christ, might be for the praise of his glory. (Ephesians 1:11–12)*

Happily ever after?

I love happy endings. When the final page is turned or closing credits roll, I'm not ashamed to admit that I want to feel good. Take a look at my home movie collection and you will discover that I purchase the films with happy endings in order to watch them over and over again. The others I just rent: once.

A film I have seen at least twenty times, *The Sound of Music*, is so good that we own two copies. Without question one of the all-time best "happily ever after" endings, the script is loosely based upon the real-life experiences of the von Trapp family. The final moments of this Hollywood classic are some of the best ever produced. Motivated by his convictions, Captain von Trapp refuses to cooperate with the Nazi regime, rejecting his commission as an officer in the Reich army. Choosing instead to flee the country with Maria and his children, he must outsmart eager and ever-watching Nazi officials. In dramatic form, they escape several close encounters—including a carefully guarded music festival, a tense church cemetery encounter with young

Rolf, and the mechanical intervention of two mischievous nuns. In the end, they are successful. As the credits role, Captain von Trapp, Maria and seven children are crossing the Swiss Alps on foot accompanied by a heavenly chorus—just the right inspiration to perfect an already magnificent climax. Could somebody please pass a tissue?

Just as happy endings dominate my home movie library, they also dominate my list of favorite Bible stories. I carry into Scripture the same desire to experience a happy ending. For example, I endure Joseph being sold into slavery and put in prison because, at the end of the story, he becomes vice-pharaoh of Egypt. After killing Goliath, David is forced to flee from the wrath of Saul into the wilderness. He did nothing wrong, and is treated like an outlaw. But I push through that portion of the drama because I know that David will eventually become king of Israel. Even the story of Job works because, after experiencing unimaginable suffering and loss, he gets back double everything he lost. In these and other stories, I find myself drawn to the ending they portray. Just like my movie collection, I return to those that satisfy— while neglecting those that don't. But we must be careful about allowing our "happily ever after" expectations to overly influence the lenses through which we see our faith lest we miss the point of the story, or more specifically, the purpose of our part.

There is a minor character in Shakespeare's *King Lear* who is so small and seemingly insignificant he is not even given a name, merely called "First Servant." His entry is a scene in which an injustice is taking place: the blinding of Gloucester. He cannot stand by and watch without challenging such cruelty, so he draws a sword and points it at his master. He is immediately stabbed from behind and killed. That is his entire part: in and out in a matter of minutes. The other characters have been part of the play from the start and will continue their roles long after his body is dragged off stage. First Servant knows very little about the larger story taking place. He only knows that in his moment he must stand for what is right. So he does, and dies. But, as C. S. Lewis reflects, if it were real life and not a play, his would be the best part to have acted because he was the only one who defended justice.

Imagine being an actor trying out for a part in King Lear. Hoping for one of the big roles, such as Lear, you are instead offered to play First Servant.

"I'm afraid we can't use you for King Lear, but we do have a part we think might fit your unique talents."

"Great! What's his name?" you ask.

"Well, he doesn't actually have a name. He is simply called 'First Servant.'"

"No name? Hmmm. Is it an important role?"

"Definitely! One of the most important."

"Terrific. Can I read through his lines?"

"Lines? Well, you won't actually have many lines. It is more of a visual, action-driven sequence."

"OK. I guess I can handle that. How many scenes?"

"One."

"Just one? Is it a big scene?"

"Well, actually, no. You enter the scene, draw a sword, and drop dead. Shouldn't take more than a few minutes total."

Hardly an actor's dream role. But as written, it is critical to the story being told.

Of course, every actor has his pride. Imagine yourself accepting the part, knowing it is beneath your acting capacity. So, rather than go with what is written, you make a few alterations that will better display your star potential. Instead of dropping dead, you make an impassioned speech and transform into Rambo in tights—stealing the scene by killing King Lear and the others on stage. The audience goes wild. You shine in the spotlight. But the story Shakespeare wanted to tell is ruined.

You and I are actors in the larger story of God. Its scenes are not ours to write or alter. We serve the drama. It doesn't serve us. We may not even understand how our part fits into the bigger picture. As Lewis put it...

> *We do not know the play. We do not know whether we are in Act I or Act V. We do not know who are the major and who the minor characters. The Author knows. The audience, if there is an audience, may have an inkling. But we, never seeing the play from outside, never meeting any characters except the tiny minority who are "on" in the same scenes as ourselves, are wholly ignorant of the future and very imperfectly informed about the past.*[54]

Our ability to accept the part written for us is critical to understanding the life of faith, particularly when, as in the case of First Servant, ours is not a "happily ever after" scene.

The story climax

Every story has a climax—that most important scene we anticipate in order to discover how it will end. As with my movie collection, we want the climax to be like *The Sound of Music*, prompting us to stand and cheer while tears of joy stream down our cheeks. But when it comes to our own real-life stories, that climax never seems to come. And for some, it feels more like a dismal tragedy than a feel-good fairy tale.

That's how it was for four young men whose lives were turned upside down when taken captive by a conquering power. Considered among the best and the brightest in Judah, Hananiah, Mishael, Azariah, and Daniel were ripped away from family and friends to spend three years training for service in the court of a foreign king. After learning the language, literature, and customs of Babylon, they received assignments and accepted their lots as glorified slaves. Having lost both freedom and their homeland, each determined to serve the new boss to the best of their abilities, trusting that God knew what He was doing.

Right from the start, it appeared they would be used to fulfill a special purpose. Though still in training, they created a scene by refusing to defile themselves with the prescribed diet. But instead of being punished, they were honored. Hard workers and diligent learners, all four rose to the top of their class. The king found them to be ten times better than any of his more experienced advisors. He gave them new names and exalted positions. Daniel, renamed Belteshazzar, saved the necks of all Babylonian wise men by fulfilling the king's command that they reveal and interpret his troubling dream, or die. He did, and was once again promoted. Clearly God had destined Daniel and his three friends for greatness.

But then things took a turn for the worse, thanks to petty jealousy and kingly arrogance. You know the story. It is found in the third chapter of the book of Daniel. The king made a 90 foot idol for everyone in the kingdom to worship, with two simple guidelines. If you bow to the idol, you live. If you refuse, you die.

Since we are told nothing about Daniel, it is assumed that he was elsewhere during this scene. But his three friends, renamed Shadrach, Meshach, and Abednego, were caught in the thick of the controversy. We enter the story right after they have been denounced for disobedience and summoned before a furious king.

> *"Is it true, Shadrach, Meshach and Abednego, that you do not serve my gods or worship the image of gold I have set up? Now when you hear the sound of the horn, flute, zither, lyre, harp, pipes and all kinds of music, if you are ready to fall down and worship the image I made, very good. But if you do not worship it, you will be thrown immediately into a blazing furnace. Then what god will be able to rescue you from my hand?" (Daniel 3:14–15)*

In the ultimate display of arrogance, King Nebuchadnezzar did more than merely order three Jews to abandon their faith. He challenged their God to do something about it. "Then what god will be able to rescue you from my hand?" came his taunt.

If you know the story, resist the temptation to rush through this scene to the ending. Camp here for a moment in order to appreciate what is about to occur. For all these three brave young men know, they are about to experience the terror of being burned alive. Yet, rather than save their own necks by caving in, they respond to the king boldly…

> "O Nebuchadnezzar, we do not need to defend ourselves
> before you in this matter. If we are thrown into the
> blazing furnace, the God we serve is able to save us
> from it, and he will rescue us from your hand, O king."
> (Daniel 3:16–17)

Again, resist the temptation to jump ahead. Remain in this scene for a moment. Shadrach, Meshach, and Abednego were not proclaiming what they expected, only what was possible. They had no more reason to expect a miracle than we would today. It had been many generations since the days of miracles. Their recent history included being enslaved by an evil, foreign power without divine intervention. If God didn't act then, why should He act now? Sure, it was possible for God to save them, but unlikely. Prompting them to add one last, very important line.

> *"But even if he does not, we want you to know, O king,*
> *that we will not serve your gods or worship the image of*
> *gold you have set up." (Daniel 3:18)*

"Even if he does not ... we will not serve your gods." Never have such potent lines been delivered, making this one of the most powerful scenes ever performed on the stage of history. You see, from the divine Author's point of view, *that* was the climax of the story! We tend to look at the next scene as the climax, when God rewards their faithfulness with rescue. But from God's perspective, the coming miracle is no big deal. It is this moment that He has been waiting for, not the next. And it has been acted to perfection. I can just imagine the Lord jumping to his feet and cheering at this point, wiping a tear from His eye and swallowing the lump in His throat.

The climax of this and other faith stories is quite different when we view them from heaven's perspective. It is not God's miraculous intervention to save the day that inspires, but rather our stubborn refusal to lose faith. Our dramatic moment comes not when all is well but when all seems lost. The most profound dramatic question is not whether God will intervene but whether we will continue holding His hand if He doesn't. Again, from God's perspective, the miracle is no big deal.

The book of Hebrews contains a portion of scripture that has been labeled "The Great Hall of Faith." It sheds light upon the real story being told, describing faith in the context of what we do not see. After summarizing the dramatic climax of many stories, including those who had experienced God's miraculous intervention, it also tells of those who did not.

> *Some faced jeers and flogging, while still others were*
> *chained and put in prison. They were stoned; they*
> *were sawn in two; they were put to death by the sword.*
> *They went about in sheepskins and goatskins, destitute,*
> *persecuted and ill-treated—the world was not worthy of*
> *them. They wandered in deserts and mountains, and in*
> *caves and holes in the ground. These were all commended*
> *for their faith, yet none of them received what had been*
> *promised. God had planned something better for us so*
> *that only together with us would they be made perfect.*
> *(Hebrews 11:36–40)*

Yes, many actors in the grand drama play parts that include wonderful scenes of divine intervention. But many others have even greater roles, like that of Shakespeare's First Servant. While they may seem minor players from our point of view, they are the true stars of time and eternity. And the day is coming when they will be recognized—when all of heaven will cheer.

From God's perspective, the climax of the story was not when Shadrach, Meshach, and Abednego walked out of the fire unharmed. It was when they walked in fully expecting to die.

The true climax of Joseph's story was not when he became vice-pharaoh. It was an earlier scene when he had every reason to question God, but refused to let go of his Maker's hand.

Job's big moment was not when he got back double everything he had lost. It was that famous scene in Job 1:21 when, having lost everything, he praised rather than cursed his God by saying, "Naked I came from my mother's womb, and naked I will depart. The Lord gave and the Lord has taken away; may the name of the Lord be praised."

These are the scenes that prompt a standing ovation in heaven. It is in such moments that the true climax of the story is understood, and when our lives most reflect the Author and ultimate hero of the grand drama.

> *Let us fix our eyes on Jesus, the author and perfecter*
> *of our faith, who for the joy set before him endured the*
> *cross, scorning its shame, and sat down at the right*
> *hand of the throne of God. Consider him who endured*
> *such opposition from sinful men, so that you will not*
> *grow weary and lose heart. (Hebrews 12:2–3)*

It was "for the joy set before him" that Jesus played a part He did not want to play. Only hours before the cross, He asked the Father to "remove this cup." But the climax of the story being told included His heroic willingness to sacrifice Himself for others. With our eternal destiny hinging upon His choice, Jesus accepted His part and acted it to perfection.

Well done!

Earlier I described one of the great happy-ending movies, *The Sound of Music*. The story is loosely based upon the true story of a man who refused to cooperate with the Nazi regime, successfully fled the country, and inspired a wonderful film. During the same era, there was another man who refused to cooperate with the Nazi regime. Despite the opportunity to "just get along" and preserve his own neck, this man actively resisted the evil that was being accepted by those around him. That man's name was Dietrich Bonhoeffer. He was a German pastor and theologian who, rather than flee the country, ended up being hanged in a German prison camp. Adding insult to injury, his death came only days before that same camp was liberated by Allied forces.

Both Captain von Trapp and Dietrich Bonhoeffer refused to cooperate with evil. Both risked everything to do what was right. One lived. The other died. You might say one got the miracle while the other did not. But, as with the three young men in Babylon and with Jesus Christ facing the cross, these stories share the same climax. It is not the ultimate outcome that defines great drama. It is the choices made.

In the famous series of letters written to his nephew, Wormwood, senior demon Screwtape responds to the junior demon's celebration over human discouragement. The elder demon knows that it is the times when human beings feel God's presence least that they are most dangerous. He writes...

> *Do not be deceived, Wormwood. Our cause is never more*
> *in danger than when a human, no longer desiring, but*
> *still intending to do our Enemy's will, looks round upon*
> *a universe from which every trace of Him seems to have*
> *vanished, and asks why he has been forsaken, and still*
> *obeys.*[55]

Our enemy does not fear the kind of faith that seeks the miracle or happy ending. What Satan fears is faith that remains strong when hope seems gone. He is terrified when we continue to trust even when feeling abandoned by God.

In his classic book *Les Misérables*, Victor Hugo reminds us that the acts of justice and charity often overlooked in this world will one day be acknowledged. "There are many of these virtues in low places..." he says, "some day they will be on high. This life has a morrow." It is only then that the true heroes of this story will be celebrated, including that eagerly anticipated moment when the Author Himself will look us in the eyes, wiping a tear from His own, and utter the words, "Well done!"

GOING DEEPER

Use the following to prompt further reflection, or to facilitate a group discussion.

Read the passage of Scripture commonly called "The Hall of Faith" in Hebrews 11:1 – 12:2 and then reflect on the following questions.

- Although much of Hebrews 11 highlights the "happy scenes" of God's redemptive story, the chapter ends with descriptions of those who suffered without experiencing rescue or a happy ending. How should knowledge of both extremes inform our own walk of faith?

- Chapter 12 describes these great men and women of faith as a "great cloud of witnesses" that inspire us to do what?

Conclusion

Awful or Good?

Scene One: I'm driving in the car with my wife of thirty years sitting beside me. Holding hands, we bask in the warmth of mutual affection, energized and refreshed by time alone together. No words need to be spoken. A small taste of heaven.

Scene Two: I'm driving in the car with my wife of thirty years sitting beside me. Refusing to touch, tension poisons the air as each stubbornly blames the other after an intense argument. No words are spoken. A small taste of hell.

Scene One has happened on countless occasions during our marriage. Scene Two could be numbered on one hand. But here we sit, stuck in rainy traffic mere inches apart, each pretending to care least while hoping the other will back down first. I would prefer a middle airplane seat nestled between complete strangers, which I hate. Why does ten hours flying over the Atlantic ignoring someone I don't know seem pleasant compared to an hour beside my soundless bride? Because, even though I dislike her at the moment, I love her. I need her. I want her. But, and this is the problem, I also blame her. Until …

"I was wrong," I mumble grudgingly.

"I know," she agrees.

"Please forgive me."

Her hand touches mine. "Of course."

Just as it is possible to experience the same person as a source of joy or a source of torment, we can experience God as either good or awful. The Scriptures describe God as a consuming fire. Fire can provide warming protection from biting cold, or scorch the careless hand. More to the point, the Scriptures describe God as a husband who invites us into intimate communion. The apostle Paul said that this God is close to each and every one of us (Acts 17:27). Welcome news if we are holding God's hand in contented silence. Otherwise, it tightens the stomach.

So we sing worship songs celebrating God's love for the world, but avoid Old Testament passages describing His wrath.

We call Him heavenly Father, yet become indignant when He does what every good dad must by telling us no.

We decry hypocritical phonies, but dislike God's policy of full disclosure about truths we wish weren't.

We expect faithful mates in marriage, but consider Christ's exclusive claim on our affections overly, well, exclusive.

We want God to author life's big story, yet chafe when we can't write, produce and star in our own play.

In short, the very same God we experience as good one moment we perceive as awful the next.

Rather than waiting in silence for God to back down or become something He isn't, maybe I should acknowledge that I am the one creating the tension between us.

Through my limited perspective obscuring the bigger picture.

By trying to define reality rather than submit to it.

With an insane belief that I know better than the One who formed and informs my mind.

That's why an outmoded word might serve me well; *Repentance* means to change one's mind and direction. To paraphrase Richard John Neuhaus, God is not fastidious about the quality of our repentance.[56] He will take what He can get, be it a reluctant mumble or an enthusiastic confession. Anything to restart the conversation.

We are made for intimacy with a God who is eager to hold our hand during the joys and struggles of life. May the reflections we've shared in these pages draw us ever closer to a Goodness whose presence, try as we might, is impossible to escape.

Notes

1   C. S. Lewis, *A Grief Observed* (New York: HarperCollins, 1996), pp. 42–43.
2   Sheldon Vanauken, *A Severe Mercy* (New York: HarperCollins, 1977), p. 186.
3   Richard John Neuhaus, *Death on a Friday Afternoon* (New York: Basic Books, 2000), p. 2.
4   Harold Kushner, *When Bad Things Happen to Good People* (New York: Avon, 1981), p. 148.
5   Neale Donald Walsch, *Conversations with God* (New York: G. P. Putnam, 1996), pp. 23–24.
6   Neuhaus, *Death on a Friday Afternoon*, p. 9.
7   Matthew 6:9–13 NKJV.
8   www.online-literature.com/george-macdonald/unspoken-sermons/31 (accessed 5.5.15).
9   Ibid.
10 Ibid.
11 Ibid.
12 Woody Allen, *Love and Death* (1975).
13 Linda Sunshine, ed., *The Illustrated Woody Allen Reader* (New York: Knopf, 1993).
14 Dorothy L. Sayers, *The Devil to Pay* (London: Victor Gollancz Ltd., 1939), p. 29.
15 Sayers, *The Devil to Pay*, p. 106.
16 John 8:3–4 HCSB.
17 John 8:4–6 HCSB.
18 John 8:7 HCSB.
19 John 8:10–11 HCSB.
20 John 8:12 HCSB.
21 John 1:9–10 HCSB.
22 John 3:19 HCSB.

23 John 3:21 HCSB.

24 J. Budziszewski, *The Revenge of Conscience* (Spence Publishing Company, Dallas 1999), p. xv.

25 Ibid., p. xiii.

26 Ibid., p. xvi.

27 Mark Twain, *The Adventures of Huckleberry Finn*, chapter 3 (London: Collins, 2010).

28 Mark Twain, *Letters from the Earth* (New York: HarperPerennial, 1991), pp. 7–8.

29 Ibid., p. 45.

30 Ibid., p. 55.

31 Ibid., p. 27.

32 Ibid., p. 49.

33 C. S. Lewis, *The Screwtape Letters* (New York: Bantam Books, 1982), p. 26.

34 Dante Alighieri, *The Inferno*, Canto XXXIV (trans. Mark Musa; New York: Penguin Books, 1984), p. 381.

35 C. S. Lewis, *Mere Christianity* (New York, Touchstone Books, 1943), p. 39.

36 Christopher Marlowe, *The Tragical History of Doctor Faustus* (London: Dent, 1937), p. 34.

37 Ibid., p. 37.

38 Ibid., p. 51.

39 Ibid., pp. 51–52.

40 Ibid., p. 96.

41 C. S. Lewis, *The Great Divorce* (New York: Simon & Schuster, 1946), p. 72.

42 Ibid., p. 96.

43 Frank McCourt, "*God in America,*" *Life* magazine (December 1998), p. 64.

44 Jeremiah Creedon, "God with a Million Faces," UTNE Reader (July/ Aug 1998), p. 42.

45 Douglas Coupland, *Life After God* (New York: Pocket Books, 1994), p. 178.

46 Coupland, *Life After God*, pp. 182–183.

47 G. K. Chesterton, *The Everlasting Man* (San Francisco, CA: Ignatius Press, 1993), pp. 248–249.

48 *Out on a Limb* directed by Robert Butler (Anchor Bay Entertainment, 1987).

49 J. R. R. Tolkien, *The Two Towers* (New York: Quality Paperback Book Club, 1995), p. 321.

50 J. R. R. Tolkien, *The Return of the King* (New York: Quality Paperback Book Club, 1995), pp. 228–229.

51 Ibid.

52 C. S. Lewis, *The Horse and His Boy* (New York: HarperCollins, 1994).

53 As paraphrased in the 2000 *Focus on the Family Radio Theatre* rendition of the original book.

54 C. S. Lewis, *The Joyful Christian* (New York: Simon & Schuster, 1977), pp. 70–71.

55 C. S. Lewis, *The Screwtape Letters* (New York: Bantam Books, 1982), p. 47.

56 Neuhaus, *Death on a Friday Afternoon*, p. 38.

Further reading

A Grief Observed by C. S. Lewis (Harper SanFrancisco)
The Problem of Pain by C. S. Lewis (Macmillan Publishing Co.)
Death on a Friday Afternoon by Richard John Neuhaus (Basic Books)
When God Doesn't Make Sense by Dr. James Dobson (Tyndale House)
Where is God When It Hurts? by Philip Yancey (Zondervan)
Disappointment with God by Philip Yancey (Zondervan)